A Friend's Guide to Chamber Music

A Friend's Guide to Chamber Music

European Trends from Haydn to Shostakovich

To Bobbi —
with appreciation!

Nancy Monsman

Nancy Monsman
Dec. 2018

CATHEDRAL ROCK ART 2018

Published by Cathedral Rock Art
Printed in the United State of America
Photography by Wilson Graham

ISBN: 978-0-692-16367-2
First Edition
This publication is made possible by a subvention from
the Arizona Friends of Chamber Music.

For information on purchasing additional copies, please contact:
Arizona Friends of Chamber Music
P.O. Box 40845
Tucson, Arizona 85717
Phone: 520-577-3769
Email: office@arizonachambermusic.org

For My Daughters

Contents

Chapter Four
The Touchstone: Beethoven's String Quartets. 62

Chapter Five
The Lyrical Romantic: Schubert's Chamber Works. 86

Chapter Six
The Romantic Poet: Schumann's Chamber Works 99

Chapter Seven
A Prodigy's Progress: Mendelssohn's Chamber Works 110

Chapter Eight
The Nostalgic Romanticist: Brahms's Chamber Works 123

Works with Varied Scoring

Chapter Nine
Czech Nationalism....................................146

Bedřich Smetana

Antonín Dvořák

Chapter Ten
Romantic Russians

Chapter Eleven
Interludes in Italy and Spain

Chapter Twelve
Diversity in Fin-de-siècle France 184

Preface

Traditionally, it's the music that speaks from the stage, not the musicians themselves. By the beginning of the 20th century, the concert hall and the music chamber were no longer regarded as appropriate venues for loud conversing, heavy drinking, reckless gambling, and high-society ogling. The concert, formerly regarded as a means of light if elegant entertainment, had become a sacred rite. Musicians and audience members alike were now expected to sit down, shut up, and focus solely and worshipfully on the music.

If you were surprised or confused by the music, nobody could help you—except the person who had written the explanatory notes in the printed program you clutched in your hands.

Today, the atmosphere is a bit more casual, though thankfully not the free-for-all it had been in the 18th century. Performers seem more relaxed; their dress is often more laid-back, their body language looser. And many of them are eager to say a few unscripted words to the audience, especially if they are introducing unfamiliar music.

Quite frequently now, an ensemble will arrive in Tucson for an Arizona Friends of Chamber Music concert expecting to give some introductory remarks about a new or unusual composition they're about to play. Then they open the printed program, read Nancy Monsman's notes, and realize that all the essential information is already there. They end up telling a couple of amusing anecdotes and urging that people learn more by reading, in their words, "the excellent notes in your programs."

I've written notes for arts presenters, record labels, and online resources, and I have strong opinions about how notes should be written. It is my strong opinion that Nancy Monsman's program notes are models of clarity and concision, providing exactly the information you need before the music takes over. When you're seated in the concert hall, waiting for the downbeat, you don't have much time to read up on what you're about to hear. There's no way you could get through a chapter of cultural background on each piece, followed by a detailed technical analysis. You need notes that, in a very few paragraphs, can set the scene for the composer and the composition, then provide just enough detail to help you find your way through the music you are about to hear.

Nancy's notes provide exactly that sort of guide. And now we are proud to present that guide in a format you can consult at your leisure, and at your pleasure, particularly if you'd like on your own to trace a composer's career more systematically than you can in a single concert. Let this be your knowledgeable companion as you explore the puzzles and delights of European chamber music.

JAMES REEL

President, Arizona Friends of Chamber Music

An Introductory Word

A Friend's Guide to Chamber Music is written for enthusiastic listeners of chamber music and also for new listeners who wish to explore this unique form—music's most democratic genre. Chamber music exists as a collaboration among equals, players who contribute their essential lines to the small group pared to fit the space of a "chamber." Since there is no conductor to impose a conception and no dominating soloist, chamber music offers an exhilarating musical discussion that delves into the creations of our most significant composers.

The *Guide* is based on my program notes written over two decades for the Arizona Friends of Chamber Music concerts, both the Evening Series and the Tucson Winter Chamber Music Festival events. For me, a "program note" is a brief written commentary that discusses the composer, important elements of his/her work, and its cultural context. In my notes I discuss key points of structure to enhance the listener's understanding of the work as performed, either in live concert or on recording. Since one hopes to demystify and enliven the composer and the work, an illuminating anecdote is a welcome find. Always, the primary purpose of the program note is to promote awareness—the key to successful listening.

The style of note writing changes continuously. During its early nineteenth-century beginnings, so many listeners both performed and experimented with composition that substantive commentary was considered unnecessary. Notes at that time tended toward biography with a few subjective comments (as "Hats off, gentlemen, a genius!"). Audiences of the early twentieth century tolerated many personal opinions from the note writer, often to the detriment of the listening experience. Today's climate is more objective. Because of the explosion of musicological research during the 1970s voluminous material exists on both the historical evolution of chamber works and their subtle technical details. *A Friend's Guide to Chamber Music* filters these resources and presents the dedicated listener with essential information in a single compendium.

True to its subtitle, the *Guide* covers European trends from Haydn's developments to the modernist works of Shostakovich. (A projected second volume would then approach more recent chamber music of the Americas and the world.) The current *Guide* discusses 175 works for three or more instruments written by 35 composers, ordered chronologically so that developments and influences can be discerned. The works have been selected from a vast repertory, and omissions are inevitable because of concerns for space. However, surveys of Beethoven's and Shostakovich's string quartets are complete, as well as both Mozart's late quartets and Brahms's chamber works for three or more instruments, because they serve as pillars for the 200 years of Western chamber music discussed.

Although I have avoided technical language, unfamiliar words or phrases might intrigue the new listener. These are briefly defined in the section of Useful Terms. Since discussions of individual composers and their works are succinct, selected readings are listed in the Sources section to provide further information.

As they say, it takes a village to raise a child, and a book requires no less. The Arizona Friends of Chamber Music deserves much gratitude for their generous support of this publication. I thank past Board President Jean-Paul Bierny for his steady encouragement. Several persons have provided astute commentary: author and AFCM Board President James Reel, Russian specialists John and Carol Garrard, Lincoln Brown, Andrea Bertassi, Wilson Graham, and my husband Gerald Monsman. Elizabeth Rosenblatt merits special acknowledgement for her careful reading and editorial insight. I especially appreciate my long and ongoing association with Jay Rosenblatt, whose keenly critical eye has been invaluable for the editorial process of this current study and past AFCM projects as well. In closing, I must thank my numerous chamber music partners, who over the years have shared inspiration and joy.

NANCY MONSMAN
Tucson, Arizona

ONE

Ingenious Origins:
Haydn's String Quartets

JOSEPH HAYDN
B. MARCH 31, 1732 IN ROHRAU, AUSTRIA,
D. MAY 31, 1809 IN VIENNA

For over two centuries composers, performers, and listeners alike have honored Haydn as "the Father of the String Quartet." His earliest efforts were simple outgrowths of the popular Baroque "trio sonata"—a form requiring four players (despite the word "trio"), two on melodic lines and two on bass. Haydn variously termed his new works "quaddro" or "divertimento." Summer employment at age twenty-three provided the catalyst for his lifelong creation in the string quartet genre. Hired by Karl Joseph Edler von Fürnberg to arrange performances for his rural Austrian castle, Haydn wrote for the available combination of players—which by chance was two violins, viola, and cello. Haydn perceived the latent possibilities of this grouping, and from that time the string quartet became his natural mode of expression. Over the course of his long career Haydn created sixty-eight string quartets that have been verified as his own and catalogued by Anthony van Hoboken (d. 1983). A selection of the forty-six quartets considered to be Haydn's mature work is reviewed in this chapter.

The Esterházy family in 1761 hired Haydn as Kapellmeister, the "chapel master" but basically composer-in-residence, and over the following twenty-nine years he wrote numerous string quartets for performances at their estates in the rural areas of Hungary and Vienna. Haydn's finely chiseled works both suited current neo-classical taste and sounded well in the resonant, heavily-marbled salons of the Esterházy. Haydn lamented his geographical distance from fellow composers but ruefully recognized the benefit of isolation; as he stated, he was "forced to become original." Fortunately, Haydn did have several stimulating meetings with Mozart during the 1780s, and the two composers developed a mutually supportive friendship. After Haydn left his Esterházy employment, he benefitted artistically from his two trips to London (1791–1792 and 1794–1795). At this late stage of his career he now conceived works for professionals performing in large concert halls rather than staff performers in small music rooms. His reputation quickly grew after these visits, and he became internationally celebrated as Europe's most important composer.

Haydn's lifelong stylistic experiments resulted in far-reaching contributions to instrumental composition. His development of the string quartet paralleled his evolution of the symphony (of which he most reliably wrote 106). Haydn solidified sonata form, the essential framework for opening movements and often subsequent ones during the Classic era and beyond. He extended variation form to enhance the slow movement; he led the evolution of the menuetto movement from a leisurely dance toward the faster scherzo; and he perfected the rondo finale form. Within these structures, Haydn continuously introduced novelty and a dramatic variety of expression that portended the Romantic movement. He set a standard for excellent craftsmanship and imaginative writing that remains today.

QUARTETS OF EARLY MATURITY (1772–1780): OPP. 20, 33, 50

Opus 20 Quartets: The "Sun" Quartets (1772)

Haydn's six revolutionary Opus 20 string quartets became known as the "Sun" Quartets after an image of a rising sun appeared on the cover of a popular early edition. Described by enthusiasts as "a sunrise over the domain of the string quartet," the Opus 20 represents a breakthrough for the medium. Haydn's earlier quartets had been scored for a dominating first violin—but in the Opus 20 all four instruments now perform as partners. Most notably the cello, liberated from its traditional bass line supporting role, plays principal themes in an expanded range. In his Opus 20 Haydn interweaves all voices in a bold and expressive manner.

Haydn composed his six Opus 20 string quartets (1772) during a period of personal restlessness that drew him to the German *Sturm und Drang* (Storm and Stress) literary movement launched by his near contemporary Johann Wolfgang von Goethe (1749–1842). Essentially a reaction to culturally dominant French rationalism, Storm and Stress literature developed with heightened passion and exuberant imagery. Inspired by Goethe's powerful language, Haydn sought to create equally expressive works. The resulting Opus 20 set reveals dramatic changes of character achieved through supple phrases intensified by bold harmonies, dramatic pauses, and unexpected turns of theme. It was rumored that Haydn, never happy in his marriage to the unmusical Maria Keller, had developed a new love interest at this time. The wide emotional range of the Opus 20 perhaps reflects both his ardor and his ambivalent state of mind.

String Quartet in C Major, Opus 20 No. 2, Hob. III:32

Moderato
Capriccio: Adagio
Menuetto: Allegretto
Fuga a quattro soggetti: Allegro

Cellists enjoy the C Major Quartet because it offers fine solo passages for the instrument, especially in the elegant opening Moderato. As a first for Haydn, the movement begins with a statement of the gracefully ornamented principal theme in the cello. The violin repeats the idea, and the cello offers a countertheme. The movement develops conversationally in sonata form.

Sturm und Drang follows in the dramatic, formally free Capriccio. Cast in C minor, this restless adagio movement begins with a bold unison declamation answered softly by the cello. Sudden shifts of tempo and dynamics convey powerful emotion throughout.

The syncopated Menuetto follows without pause. A sustained drone note in the first section whimsically suggests a bagpipe; the contrasting trio section (C minor) showcases the cello. The Allegro finale, marked "always in a quiet voice," is an ingenious fugue with four subjects. Near its conclusion the dynamic marking changes to forte, and the figuration becomes ever more rapid. In the manuscript Haydn writes a humorous twist on the meaning of "fugue" as "imitative chase": "Praise the Lord. Thus one friend flees another friend."

String Quartet in F Minor, Opus 20 No. 5, Hob. III:35

Allegro moderato
Menuetto
Adagio
Finale: Fuga a due soggetti

Opus 20 No. 5, one of Haydn's few works in the minor key, has been described as the most intensely expressive quartet that he ever wrote. The darkly melancholy Allegro moderato develops two themes—a haunting primary theme stated by the first violin over a steadily pulsing accompaniment, and a warmer second idea (D flat major) shared by all the instruments. The two motifs are extended and led through remote modulations until their resolution at the dramatic coda. The somber Menuetto (F minor) is varied by a more cheerful trio section (F major). The serene Adagio (F major) resembles a *siciliano*, a pastoral Italian dance; its opening melody, heard in the first violin, is inventively embellished throughout.

A contrapuntal tour de force, the Finale (Fugue with Two Subjects) first introduces the motif "And with His Stripes" from Handel's *Messiah*; the complementary second theme that follows moves with faster note values as a countersubject. The majority of the movement is marked *sotto voce* (in an undertone) until a sudden forceful statement shatters the quiet spell. A canonic passage between the violin and cello brings the movement to a powerful conclusion.

Opus 33 Quartets: Gli Scherzi (1781)

Haydn wrote the six quartets of his Opus 33 during the especially productive year of 1781. It was reported that he then radiated good cheer, perhaps because he had recently renegotiated his contract with the Esterházys, who formerly held full rights to his compositions, and could now publish works as his own. The Opus 33 quartets were originally known as "The Russian" because Haydn dedicated them to the Grand Duke Paul of Russia, who hosted their premiere on Christmas Day. However, Haydn's amiable Opus 33 is generally known as *Gli Scherzi*, an Italian term that puns on its dual translation as "the jokes," a reference to the humorous qualities of these quartets, and "the scherzos," Haydn's new term for his light and accelerated menuetto movements. Written after a ten-year hiatus from quartet composition, these works were described by Haydn as being written "in a new and special way." He termed his new technique "thematic elaboration," a process by which the music develops not by the restatement of complete subjects but rather by the manipulation of short motifs derived from a movement's initial ideas. In Opus 33 these motifs are distributed throughout all four voices so that the instruments alternately assume leading and subordinate roles. The resulting equality among the players inspired Goethe's famous comparison of the string quartet form to "a conversation among four intelligent people." Opus 33 strongly impacted Mozart and Beethoven, both of whom modelled quartets on these inventive works.

String Quartet in E flat Major, Opus 33 No. 2, Hob. III:38 ("The Joke")

Allegro moderato
Scherzando: Allegro
Largo sostenuto
Finale: Presto

Each of the Opus 33 quartets has its own nickname, affectionately bestowed by listeners rather than Haydn himself. The E flat Major Quartet has been identified as "The Joke" because of its droll finale—which at several points appears to end but then recommences. The story goes that Haydn here interpolated unexpected rests in order to expose certain audience members who rudely talked during his performances.

The first three movements unfold with subtle wit. The expansive Allegro moderato develops its two related themes entirely from small gestures heard in its opening measures. Marked "singing," this genial movement most probably influenced Mozart's K. 428 Quartet (E flat major, 1783), one of the six that he dedicated to Haydn. As in his earlier menuetto forms, Haydn uses material that suggests Austrian folk music in the three-part scherzo movement, which opens and concludes with a rustic dance; a lilting middle section provides contrast. The expressive center of the quartet falls in the serene Largo (B flat major), an extended song varied through duet and trio scorings. The Presto finale is a *tarantella*, a vigorous Italian dance with humorous rests and resets that later made even the reserved Clara Schumann laugh.

String Quartet in G Major, Opus 33 No. 5, Hob. III:41 ("Compliments")

Vivace assai
Largo e cantabile
Scherzo: Allegro
Finale: Allegretto

The fifth quartet of the Opus 33 set has been named "Compliments" because early listeners heard courtly graciousness in the upward-moving flourishes of its animated Vivace assai. (Perhaps as homage, Beethoven's Haydn-inspired Opus 18 No. 3 Quartet in the identical G major key received the same nickname.) Rests that mimic conversational pauses articulate the sonata form structure of this vivacious movement.

The G minor slow movement is a rhapsodic statement for violin accompanied by the other instruments. Its extended cadenza is answered by an abrupt unison statement from the other instrument, as if to say "Enough!" A solitary pizzicato note punctuates the final measure.

Surprising metrical displacements in the first violin line create a playful atmosphere for the Scherzo. The Finale, so popular that Haydn created a piano version for it, consists of a genial theme with five variations.

Opus 50 Quartets: The "Prussian" (1784–1787)

Haydn profited uniquely from the musical interests of Frederick William of Prussia, nephew and successor to the flute-playing Frederick II ("The Great"). An accomplished cellist and avid quartet player, Frederick William invited Europe's most significant composers to contribute works for his Berlin court performances. Frederick William commissioned a memorial cantata from Haydn for his uncle's funeral, and after his coronation he requested a selection of other works. Haydn sent the newly-crowned king his set of six "Paris" symphonies together with the promise to create for him six string quartets. The king responded by sending Haydn a diamond ring "as a sign of my satisfaction and the good grace of my disposition." Haydn regarded the ring as a source of inspiration and wore it whenever he composed.

The six Opus 50 string quartets, completed for Frederick William at the midpoint of Haydn's quartet production, are often called the "Prussian Quartets." The influence of Mozart, with whom Haydn had a mutually inspiring relationship, is reflected in their increased intensity of expression and novel approaches to form and texture. In his Opus 50 quartets Haydn experimented with essentially monothematic writing in which all secondary subjects are derived from the first thematic idea. The result is a high degree of unity and balance in the quartets.

String Quartet in F Major, Opus 50 No. 5, Hob. III:48 ("The Dream")

Allegro moderato
Poco adagio
Tempo di Menuetto: Allegretto
Finale: Vivace

Opus 50 No. 5, the last of the "Prussian" Quartets to be completed, is among the most concise of the set, perhaps because Haydn's publishers were pressuring him for its submission. The opening Allegro moderato, in sonata form, conversationally develops its ideas from the germinal motif introduced in the vigorous opening duet between the two violins. Sudden pauses set off the various sections of this effervescent movement.

Nineteenth-century listeners gave Opus 50 No. 5 the title *Der Traum* ("The Dream") because of its ethereal second movement, which conjures the sustained weightlessness of a dream. All four instruments weave together a rich fabric in this two-part movement (exposition and recapitulation, B flat major). The Menuetto, in traditional three-part form, is animated by persistent turn figures and varied by a minor-key trio section. The final Vivace, which develops with surprising harmonic twists, brings the work to a spirited conclusion.

String Quartet in D Major, Opus 50 No. 6, Hob. III:49 ("The Frog")

Allegro
Poco adagio
Menuetto: Allegretto
Allegro con spirito

The most famous quartet of the Opus 50 set, Quartet No. 6 in D Major opens with a terse statement that is fragmented, freely modified, and ingeniously developed to create a restless and dramatic sonata form movement. Also written in sonata form, the D minor Poco adagio develops an eloquent song through inventive harmonic treatment; its florid cello line was doubtless crafted to please cellist Frederick William. The three-part Menuetto begins with a forceful section followed by a gentler trio. Tentative pauses signal a repeat of the opening section.

Quartet No. 6 is popularly known as "The Frog" because of the distinctive timbre created by single-pitch legato duplets played sequentially on two adjacent strings. Nineteenth-century listeners, not Haydn, thought that this humorous recurring pattern suggested pond life, and the nickname has continued.

THE MIDDLE QUARTETS:
OPP. 54, 55, 64, "TOST" QUARTETS (1788–1790)

Haydn dedicated his twelve "middle period" string quartets— three each in Opp. 54 and 55, and six in Opus 64—to the virtuoso Johann Tost, principal violinist of the Esterházy orchestra. It is testimony to Haydn's generous and forgiving nature that the somewhat unscrupulous Tost received such a magnificent tribute. After his auspicious engagement to an Esterházy cousin, Tost began to anticipate his retirement. As a gesture to his longtime colleague Haydn, Tost promised to find a publisher for him in Paris. He was successful in placing the six Opus 54 and 55 scores as well as two Haydn symphonies—together with a Gyrowitz symphony that he passed off as one of Haydn's. Although these works were soon published, Tost slowly sent only partial payments to Haydn. Upon his return to Vienna Tost set himself up as a cloth merchant. He then played violin solely for amusement until business reverses forced his return to orchestra performance.

Each of Haydn's middle period quartets reveals new stylistic refinements. Perhaps inspired by the six outstanding quartets that Mozart had recently dedicated to him, Haydn now resolved to contribute only works of exquisite polish to the quartet literature. Every work can be heard as a brilliant conversation among the four instruments, each introducing important ideas and developing them with supple phrases that demand technical skill.

String Quartet in C Major, Opus 54 No. 2, Hob. III:57

Vivace
Adagio
Menuetto: Allegretto
Finale: Adagio—Presto—Adagio

The String Quartet in C Major (1788), the second of the three Opus 54 quartets, is considered the most intensely expressive and imaginative of the set. Its dramatic pauses and abrupt changes of tempo, indicative of Haydn's ongoing experiments with structure, anticipate gestures heard in the late opus quartets of Beethoven.

The opening Vivace develops its two contrasting themes with intriguing shifts of tonality. Virtuoso writing for the first violin, heard in each of these middle period quartets, suggests Tost's superb skill as a performer. The Adagio (C minor) opens with a solemn theme intoned in the instruments' low registers. After three repetitions of the theme, the first violin weaves rhapsodic arabesques over sustained harmonies in the other strings. The delightful Menuetto (C major) proceeds without pause. This movement so charmed Prince Nikolaus Esterházy, Haydn's last employer, that he incorporated its theme into the mechanism of his musical clock. After a bold trio section (Allegretto), the Menuetto returns.

Normally a rapid movement, the Finale is unusual for its predominantly slow tempo. After a short introduction, the violin introduces a serene and noble theme, which is briefly interrupted by a Presto section that recalls the opening Vivace. The Adagio sections are notable for their wide-ranging cello lines, stately ascensions of arpeggios moving from the lowest C through three and a half octaves.

String Quartet in D Major, Opus 64 No. 5, Hob. III:63 ("Lark")

Allegro moderato
Adagio: Cantabile
Menuetto: Allegretto
Finale: Vivace

The "Lark" Quartet (1790), the fifth of the Opus 64 set, was written during a month of rapidly changing life circumstances for Haydn. His employer, Nikolaus Esterházy, had recently died, and Haydn found himself free to pursue his own musical career after nearly thirty years of service. At the urging of the impresario Johann Peter Salomon, he quickly arranged a trip to London, where he knew he had ardent musical supporters—some so zealous that a plot once existed to kidnap Haydn from his unappreciative employer and transport him to England.

The nickname "Lark" did not originate with Haydn but rather with listeners who associated a bird's soaring flight with the opening violin melody. The first movement is notable for its exquisite diversity of thematic development. Its two genial themes are transformed into darker, mysterious statements through dissonances, syncopations and changes of register before the movement's joyous recapitulation.

The profoundly expressive Adagio cantabile, made poignant through its appoggiaturas and chromatic tones, resembles an extended operatic aria for violin. The robust Menuetto is interrupted by a contrasting trio section in the minor key; the vigorous opening material then returns. The rapid finale consists of two D major sections in a soft dynamic range alternating with a robust D minor section. Since at moments the movement suggests an English hornpipe, it is probable that Haydn created it with his London audience in mind.

THE LATE QUARTETS (1793–1799)

Opus 71 and Opus 74: The "Apponyi" Quartets (1793)

During his twenty-nine-year career as Kapellmeister to the Esterházy family, Haydn rarely traveled outside the summer and winter estates of these essentially rural nobles. After he resigned from his position in 1790, he happily accepted an invitation from impresario Johann Salomon to concertize in London, where his fame was enormous. Haydn was greatly impressed by the experience of hearing professional concerts in London's large public halls, a major change of venue from the remote Esterházy music rooms staffed by servant-performers. Soon after his return to Vienna, where he now lived as an independent composer, Haydn was befriended by Count Anton Georg Apponyi, a generous Hungarian diplomat. Apponyi urged him to join his own Brotherhood of Masons and also to write (for a handsome fee) six string quartets that would bear his name. Haydn declined the fraternal offer but accepted the commission, and in 1793 he composed the quartets—divided as three each in Opus 71 and Opus 74. Since he was then preparing a program for his second visit to London, Haydn wrote the quartets for the concert hall rather than the Count's intimate salon.

Influenced by orchestral sonorities, these quartets signal a transformation in Haydn's chamber style. As in his "London" symphonies of the same period, the quartets feature slow introductions, virtuoso part-writing and memorably tuneful melodies. Their intense expressiveness, conveyed through bold harmonic modulations and strong dynamic contrasts, signals Haydn's steady development towards Romanticism.

String Quartet in D Major, Opus 71 No. 2, Hob. III:70

Adagio—Allegro
Adagio cantabile
Menuetto: Allegro
Finale: Allegretto—Allegro

Opus 71 No. 2 requires the full ensemble's utmost technical prowess because of its rapid unison passages and intricate thematic dovetailing. After a brief introduction that both offers a reverent hint of a British hymn and anticipates the principal theme, the Allegro proceeds without pause. This energetic sonata form movement exploits a clearly chiseled motif and a related secondary idea to suggest a mischievous chase. The noble Adagio unfolds in three-part song form; its main theme, heard in the violin, is complemented by rhapsodic cello arabesques. The brief and lively Menuetto, introduced by a low-register cello motif, is varied by a lilting trio section at its center. The Finale is an energetic rondo based on an infectious theme that suggests British folk dance; grace notes in the upper strings contribute piquancy. In the final section the tempo accelerates and all four players execute virtuoso passagework.

String Quartet in C Major, Op. 74 No. 1, Hob. III:72

Allegro moderato
Andantino grazioso
Menuetto: Allegretto
Finale: Vivace

Opus 74 No. 1, the fourth Apponyi Quartet (1793), opens with two introductory chords followed by an extensive statement enlivened by expressive chromaticism—sinuous half-step motion that is heard throughout the entire quartet. The second theme is a similarly chromatic idea derived from the first motif; both themes are developed with rapid and intricate passagework.

The songful Andantino grazioso (G major) suggests the influence of Mozart, with whom Haydn had a mutually nurturing relationship. Its two graceful themes are developed in leisurely sonata form. The brisk Menuetto (C major) is notable for its bold harmonic movement to A major in the trio section, an Austrian tune played *mezza voce*, or in half voice. A movement that demands virtuosity from all players, the Finale is a vivacious sonata-rondo. Its incisively witty main theme is enlivened by vigorous imitation among all voices in its development and the occasional droll suggestion of a bagpipe.

String Quartet in G Minor, Opus 74 No. 3, Hob. III:74 ("Rider")

Allegro
Largo assai
Menuetto—Allegretto
Finale: Allegro con brio

Opus 74 No. 3 (1793) has been nicknamed "The Rider" because of the vigorous rhythmic figuration in both its first and final movements. The Allegro's opening theme, based on an arpeggio figure, is followed by a second idea based on a rocking triplet rhythm. This energetic second idea begins to dominate the movement as the lilting first theme gradually recedes. Typical of his late works, Haydn explores bold key relationships but somewhat prepares his listener; the G minor opening movement (two flat notes) concludes in G major (one sharp) as a transition to the following E major Largo (four sharp notes).

The Largo assai, written in three-part song form, achieved fame through its five piano transcriptions. This profound movement, varied by an ethereal central section in the minor mode, unfolds with expressive chromaticism that portends the coming Romantic era. The Menuetto, based on an Austrian dance tune, moves with skillful counterpoint. A movement of exhilarating drive, the finale develops two energetic themes.

Opus 76: The Erdődy Quartets (1796–1797, published 1799)

Haydn wrote his Opus 76 set of six string quartets as a commission for Count Joseph Erdődy, a Hungarian aristocrat who was also an early supporter of Beethoven. Haydn had recently returned from his second immensely successful visit to London, where he was lionized as Europe's greatest living composer—an accurate assessment, since Mozart had died five years earlier and Beethoven had not yet established his reputation. Although Haydn had composed quartets for forty years, his Opus 76 set reveals new confidence. Greater technical assurance is evident in the profound slow movements, energetic menuetto movements, and intellectually challenging finales of Opus 76. Because of the high level of workmanship in these imaginative quartets, Opus 76 is considered to be a peak of eighteenth-century chamber music.

String Quartet in G Major, Opus 76 No. 1, Hob. III:75

Allegro con spirito
Adagio sostenuto
Menuetto; Presto
Allegro ma non troppo

The emphatic three-chord opening to Opus 76 No. 1 suggests an orchestral fanfare. The Allegro con spirito then introduces two themes that undergo fragmentation and inventive recombination as the movement develops. The warmly romantic Adagio sostenuto (C major) expressively develops three ideas—a chorale theme heard in all instruments; a dialogue between the first violin and viola; and a violin line accompanied by short, repeated notes in the other instruments.

The rapid Menuetto anticipates the energetic scherzo movements of Beethoven; its slower central section suggests Austrian folk influence. The Finale, which begins in the key of G minor, recalls Haydn's early "storm and stress" movements until its cheerful G major recapitulation and coda.

String Quartet in D Minor, Opus 76 No. 2, Hob. III:76 ("Fifths")

Allegro
Andante o più tosto allegretto
Menuetto: Allegro ma non troppo
Finale: Vivace assai

Opus 76 No. 2 has been nicknamed "Quinten" or "Fifths" because of the paired descending intervals of the fifth heard at its beginning and repeated over eighty times throughout the first movement. Since the opening four bars also resemble the melody marking the quarter hours of Big Ben, a familiar London landmark for Haydn, the quartet has also been nicknamed "The Bells."

The graceful Andante (D major) unfolds in a three-part design. The violin states the opening melody, which appears in the minor key in the middle section and returns with embellishments in the final part. The intricate Menuetto (D minor), known as the "Witches' Minuet," opens as a canon—the violins begin the melody, which three beats later is imitated an octave lower by the viola and cello to create the illusion of a ghostly echo. As a contrast, the major-mode trio section moves with chords that change dynamic level from very soft to very loud. The sonata form Finale develops with syncopated rhythms and pungent intervals that capture the spirit of Hungarian folk music.

*String Quartet in C Major, Opus 76 No 3, Hob. III:77
("Emperor")*

Allegro
Poco adagio; cantabile (Variations)
Menuetto: Allegro
Finale: Presto

The name "Emperor" was bestowed on Opus 76 No. 3 because of its expressive second movement, based on the hymn that Haydn had written in 1797 to honor Emperor Franz II of Austria on his birthday. This hymn, *Gott erhalte Franz den Kaiser* ("God Protect Emperor Franz"), eventually became Austria's national anthem as well as a popular religious hymn. A piano transcription of this noble movement was the final music that Haydn chose to play at the end of his life.

The opening Allegro, in sonata form, develops a single theme through ingenious transformations. The renowned theme of the second movement (G major) undergoes four variations, each of which retains the hymn's basic identity. Initially stated by the first violin, the theme passes to the second violin, followed by the cello and viola, as the other instruments articulate countermelodies. All instruments join the statement of the profound final variation.

The Menuetto is a rustic dance with a quieter contrasting trio section. The energetic sonata form Finale develops two motifs—an emphatic group of three chords and a lyrical response that recalls the opening movement.

String Quartet in B flat Major, Opus 76 No. 4, Hob. III:78 ("Sunrise")

Allegro con spirito
Adagio
Menuetto: Allegro
Finale: Allegro ma non troppo

The name "Sunrise" for Opus 76 No. 4 arose from the opening notes of the first movement—the first violin articulates an ascending arc above a sustained chord in the other strings to conjure the visual image of a rising sun. This motif and two new contrasting ideas are developed in sonata form with ingenious harmonies and a spirited conclusion. The Adagio, written at a continuously soft dynamic level relieved by occasional accents, is a free fantasia based on the quartet's opening "Sunrise" motif. The Menuetto, a rustic dance with much rhythmic verve, also develops a motif based on this introductory theme. Its heavily accented trio, accompanied by a drone bass, suggests Balkan folk music. The melody developed in the vivacious Finale is believed to be an adaptation of an English folk song. At the coda the tempo accelerates to a swift conclusion on a succession of B flat major chords.

String Quartet in D Major, Opus 76 No. 5, Hob. III:79

Allegretto
Largo: Cantabile e mesto
Menuetto: Allegro
Finale: Presto

By the time Haydn composed his Opus 76 quartets, he was beginning to experiment with first movements that deviated from established classical sonata form. In Opus 76 No. 5 the opening Allegretto consists of three sections delineated by D major-D minor-D major key areas; a substantial coda (Allegro) follows. Graceful and inventive variations of the pastoral theme occur within each section.

The Largo develops two broadly singing themes in the remote key of F sharp major (six sharps), a strong harmonic contrast to the opening movement. First heard in the violin, the motifs are taken up by the other instruments and transformed into ethereal statements with myriad tone colors.

Unexpected accents enliven the Menuetto (D major). The D minor trio section features a sinuous cello statement, to which the other instruments reply; the Menuetto returns with a full repeat.

After a brief fanfare, the first violin introduces the playful first theme of the Presto finale; the cello echoes the idea. The two themes of this buoyant, virtuoso movement are developed with unexpected turns of harmony and rhythm.

Opus 77: The "Lobkowitz" Quartets (1799)

Two stories surround the origin of Haydn's Opus 77, his last completed string quartets. According to the first anecdote, Prince Lobkowitz, who commissioned the two Opus 77 quartets, actually desired string quintets in the manner of Mozart, who had died eight years earlier. Haydn demurred, insisting that he did not wish to place himself in competition with a composer of such sublime and perfect works. Lobkowitz persisted. When Haydn eventually presented him with a manuscript for string quartets with blank fifth lines, the Prince exclaimed, "My dear Haydn, you have forgotten the fifth part!" Haydn replied, "No, your Highness, I have left it for you to fill up. You can do it better than I."

According to the second story, Lobkowitz commissioned both Haydn and the young Beethoven to write string quartets for his palace concerts. Haydn had intended to write six quartets for his Opus 77 set, but when he realized that the audience favored

Beethoven's efforts, he decided to stop after two. However, it is certain that Haydn's main preoccupation at this time was not the string quartet but rather the completion of his final great masses and oratorios. It is also a certainty that the sophisticated craftsmanship of Opus 77 exerted a profound influence on the young Beethoven.

String Quartet in F Major, Opus 77 No. 2, Hob. III: 82

Allegro moderato
Menuetto: Presto, ma non troppo
Andante
Finale: Vivace assai

Surprises are continuously introduced into each movement of Opus 77 No. 2—unexpected rests, offbeat entrances, unusual key relationships. The opening movement, in sonata form, explores two themes—a principal idea based on the descending F major scale and a contrasting second motif initially accompanied by the second violin playing the opening theme. Its substantial development section closes with a measure of silence, and the movement ends with a brief recapitulation of the two themes. Roguish and inventive, the Menuetto juggles two-against-three rhythmic patterns; its central trio section provides a subdued contrast. The Andante offers three freely structured variations of an expressive theme. The vigorous Finale suggests Hungarian folk dance.

TWO

A Classical Peak:
Mozart's Chamber Works

WOLFGANG AMADEUS MOZART
B. JANUARY 27, 1756 IN SALZBURG, AUSTRIA,
D. DECEMBER 5, 1791 IN VIENNA

A phenomenal prodigy, Mozart as a young child was shaped by his father Leopold, a composer with strong German grounding and a teacher renowned for his *Violinschule*, a popular instruction book. Leopold groomed his son for a career in one of Europe's important courts, a goal that never materialized. Yet the father and his fragile son persistently traveled to numerous musical centers—Munich, Vienna, Paris, Versailles, London, and three times to aristocratic circles in Italy—in hopes of a court appointment. Despite disappointments, the artistic benefit of these restless trips was enormous. Wolfgang heard distinct stylistic elements in each region he visited: the varied lyricism of the Italians, the elegant precision of the French, the structural solidity of the Germans. Possessed of a flawless aural memory, he retained all diverse impressions and fused them in his compositions over the following decades of his brief life. He then created an international style that is a hallmark of high Classicism—an era of clarity and refinement that flourished during the latter years of the eighteenth century.

STRING QUARTETS

The "Haydn" Quartets (1782–1785)

Mozart had admired Haydn's early quartets during his youthful travels to Vienna, and the master's ingenious techniques influenced his own composition. Soon after Mozart settled permanently in Vienna in 1781, he and Haydn began to perform together at quartet parties, informal musical evenings hosted by fellow composers to critique and enjoy each other's new works. At several sessions Mozart performed and examined the scores for Haydn's provocative Opus 33 Quartets *Gli Scherzi* (The Jokes, 1781)—six works described by their composer as "written in a new, very special manner." Impressed by their seemingly effortless technique and wit, Mozart began to rethink his own methods of quartet composition, a form he had neglected for over a decade. In his first sixteen string quartets Mozart had composed by recasting successions of full melodies, most scored for first violin. Inspired by the Opus 33, Mozart now explored shorter melodic units that could be shared by all players. Following Haydn's process of "thematic elaboration," he created supple forms that developed organically through the manipulation of short motifs derived from subjects introduced at the beginnings of movements. Since Mozart now heard the instruments as equally important voices, his string quartets no longer resembled lightly accompanied violin concerti.

Between 1782 and 1785 Mozart wrote a set of six boldly innovative quartets that he termed "the fruit of long, arduous labor." He dedicated the set to Haydn, "from whom I learned to write quartets," and Haydn pronounced them a resounding success. After hearing the first three of the new quartets, Haydn proclaimed to Mozart's father Leopold: "Before God and as an honest man, I tell you that your son is the greatest composer known to me either in person or by name. He has taste, and what is more, the most profound knowledge of composition." Viennese reaction was unfortunately muted, and the quartets did not lead to the commissions that Mozart desired. However, the "Haydn" Quartets profoundly influenced Beethoven, who closely studied Mozart's scores and used them as models for his own chamber compositions.

String Quartet in G Major, K. 387

Allegro vivace assai
Menuetto: Allegro
Andante cantabile
Molto allegro

Mozart doubtless considered K. 387 (1782), the first of the "Haydn" Quartets, to be a significant homage to Haydn—it offers the innovative thematic development, fugal moments, and overall atmosphere of delight heard in Haydn's *Gli Scherzi* (which also begins with a quartet in G major). K. 387's four movements are unified by two pervasive gestures first heard in its opening four measures: the abrupt alternation of piano and forte to achieve dramatic contrast; and the weaving of chromatic (half step) scale fragments into the melodic line to create subtle changes of mood.

The three themes of the Menuetto (G major with a contrasting G minor trio section) are not merely repeated, as is customary in this generally easygoing movement, but are developed in classical sonata form so that the movement achieves weight and significance. The Andante cantabile movement (C major) also develops three themes, each explored through an outpouring of melody that is alternately intense and serene. Mozart's wife Constanze much admired the effervescent finale (G major), which features fugal techniques that he had learned through earlier studies of Haydn's Opus 20 Quartets. In his Molto allegro Mozart ingeniously combines contrapuntal passages and tuneful homophonic areas within a classical sonata framework. The important first theme is based on a four-note motif that Mozart later used in the last movement of the "Jupiter" Symphony.

String Quartet in D Minor, K. 421

Allegro moderato
Andante
Menuetto: Allegretto
Allegretto ma non troppo

Constanze Mozart wrote that her husband began K. 421, the second of his "Haydn" Quartets, during the labor and birth of their first child, Raimund Leopold, on June 17, 1783. Mozart sat in the adjacent room and occasionally visited Constanze to give comfort. Despite a biographer's judgment of Mozart's behavior as "the callousness of genius," the manuscript does contain enough erasures and corrections to indicate frequent interruptions.

The passionate Allegro develops its two themes with bold harmonic changes. At the end of the exposition, the violin plays a motto that ends with three repeated notes, an idea that is heard in each of the following movements. The three-part Andante, a somber movement with an undercurrent of agitation, exploits this motto in its middle section. Many listeners claim to detect the cries of Constanze in its abruptly forceful cello passages.

The Menuetto, largely based on the three-note motto, projects a serious atmosphere, but its trio section (D major) provides a lighter contrast. The substantial finale (D minor) consists of four variations based on the *siciliano*, a pastoral Italian rhythm. A faster coda (Più allegro) brings the work to a brisk conclusion.

String Quartet in E flat Major, K. 428

Allegro non troppo
Andante con moto
Menuetto: Allegro
Allegro vivace

Mozart began K. 428, his third "Haydn" Quartet, during the days following the birth of his short-lived first son in June 1783. The first movement intricately develops two deceptively simple motifs—the first, distinguished by its initial octave leap, is played in unison by all instruments; the calmer second idea, heard four bars later, is energized by a rhythmic figure in the second violin. The pungent dissonances heard in the Andante con moto (A flat major) have led to comparisons with Wagner's rich and daring harmonies—a late Romantic sound world that was realized seven decades later. The large upward leaps of the vigorous Menuetto (E flat major) echo the opening motif of the first movement. A central trio section (G minor) provides contrast. The finale of K. 428 is a good-natured rondo (E flat major) with three repetitions of the main theme. Unexpected silences and surprising dynamic contrasts suggest the sly wit of Joseph Haydn.

String Quartet in B flat Major, K. 458 ("Hunt")

Allegro vivace assai
Menuetto: Moderato
Adagio
Allegro assai

The popular favorite of all the "Haydn" Quartets, Mozart's good-natured K. 458 achieves a satisfying four-part discourse that resembles, in Goethe's words, "a conversation among four intelligent people." Thematic fragments circulate among the players to suggest witty repartee. Its subtitle "Hunt" was not coined by Mozart but rather by nineteenth-century listeners who heard hunting horn fanfares at its opening. In fact, the simple horns of Mozart's day would have performed in K. 458's key of B flat major.

The buoyant first movement is structurally remarkable because its two contrasting themes are developed primarily in the recapitulation and the lengthy coda rather than in the brief development section itself. The Menuetto (B flat major), in a moderate tempo, suggests a stately dance animated by off-beat accents; the buoyant trio, also in B flat major, provides thematic contrast. The substantial Adagio (E flat major) develops two richly expressive themes with subtle chromaticism and elegantly restrained ornamentation. The Allegro assai, which re-establishes the lively mood of the opening, develops three themes suggesting Austrian folk influence.

String Quartet in A Major, K. 464 ("The Drum")

Allegro
Menuetto
Andante
Allegro non troppo

Mozart wrote K. 464 (1785), the fifth of his "Haydn" Quartets, while completing the "Hunt" Quartet (K. 458) and conceptualizing his "Dissonant" Quartet (K. 465). His A Major Quartet has been nicknamed "The Drum" because of the military tattoo effect heard in the cello near the conclusion of the Andante. This unique sonority caught the young Beethoven's attention as he was preparing to write his Opus 18 string quartets fifteen years later; his own A Major Quartet, also the fifth of a set, develops with numerous references to Mozart's K. 464, especially its theme and variations third movement.

Three deceptively simple themes are introduced at the outset of the opening Allegro. Constructed with intricate inner motives and beguiling inflections of the minor mode, these themes and their implications are fully explored in the substantial development section. Passages of counterpoint enliven the recapitulation. The movement closes with a subtle codetta in which soft and loud dynamics alternate to emphasize the varied rhythms of the concluding motives.

The Menuetto continues the scheme of alternating loud-soft dynamics. The first motive is played in unison by all instruments; the harmonized second idea is launched by three staccato note repetitions. The trio section (E major) offers a warmly flowing contrast.

The Andante (D major), which won the acclaim of Beethoven, explores a strongly profiled theme through six increasingly complex variations. The final variation is underpinned by emphatic staccato figuration, first heard in the cello and then in the viola, to conjure a military drummer.

The ebullient Allegro non troppo is based on a central theme heard initially in the violin. This idea is expanded by all instruments and supported by rhythmic undercurrents that suggest distant drumrolls. The movement concludes with a quiet hush.

String Quartet in C Major, K. 465 ("Dissonant")

Adagio—Allegro
Andante cantabile
Menuetto: Allegro
Allegro

Mozart wrote K. 465, the last of his "Haydn" Quartets, in 1785. Its remarkable twenty-two measure Adagio introduction was at that time a daring harmonic experiment. This highly chromatic and harmonically unstable passage disconcerted eighteenth-century concertgoers (as well as Haydn), and it became nicknamed "Dissonant"; however, the passage fascinated Beethoven, who explored similar progressions in his own quartets. At the Allegro the key of C major is immediately established, and the lively themes of this sonata form movement appear even more lucid because of the tonally obscure beginning.

The Andante cantabile (F major) develops two themes—a lyrical idea that is shaped by contributions from all four instruments and a more declamatory statement that becomes an ardent dialogue between the first violin and cello. After a recapitulation of these ideas, the viola offers a new countermelody to this duet. Abrupt changes of dynamics, unexpected rests, and poignant chromatic fragments dramatize this engaging movement.

The good-natured Menuetto is energized by sudden contrasts of dynamics and articulation. The long-arched melodies of its passionate trio section (C minor) provide dramatic contrast; the C major Menuetto section is then restated.

The robust Allegro, cast in sonata rondo form, opens with an incisive theme that is varied with brilliant passagework at its several returns. New ideas enhanced by chromaticism appear throughout this delightful movement. This finale is especially notable for its substantial coda; here Mozart introduces a motif that he had previously borrowed from Gluck for a set of piano variations, as well as a slow trill-like sequence that he later used in his opera *Così fan tutte*.

String Quartet in D Major, K. 499 ("Hoffmeister")

Allegretto
Menuetto: Allegretto
Adagio
Allegro

Mozart composed 23 string quartets over the course of his career, but the final ten quartets are considered his greatest achievements in the form. The first six were influenced by Joseph Haydn, whose own quartets had brought Mozart back to the medium, and the final three "Prussian" Quartets were conceived for Friedrich Wilhelm II, the cello-playing King of Prussia. Between these sets Mozart departed from the eighteenth-century custom of composing quartets in groups and created K. 499 (1786), which stands alone. He subtitled the quartet "Hoffmeister" to honor his friend, the composer and publisher Franz Anton Hoffmeister, but it is not known if he wrote the work to fill a commission, to repay a debt, or simply as a gesture of appreciation. Compared to his nine other late quartets, the "Hoffmeister" Quartet is a more personally indulgent exploration of sensuously beautiful texture and harmony.

Although the Allegretto opens with a buoyant theme that promises light entertainment, this richly complex movement continuously deepens as it progresses. Three subsequent motifs are dramatically developed through contrapuntal dialogues between the instruments and strong contrasts of dynamics and texture.

The songful Menuetto (D major) unfolds with imitative motivic treatment, expressive chromaticism, and a robust dynamic level. The trio (D minor), somber despite its energetic triplet figures, also develops imitatively. A repeat of the Menuetto concludes the movement.

The expressive weight of the quartet falls in the expansive Adagio, a classically balanced A-B-A form movement that suggests a grouping of glorious arias. Opening in G major, the harmonies soon modulate to remote areas poignantly colored by expressive chromaticism.

The brightly virtuoso Allegro finale, in sonata form, begins with fragmented statements of a whimsical motif that merge into a full line as all the instruments enter. The abrupt rests, perhaps homage to the surprise-loving Haydn, contribute an element of humor. The violins introduce the complementary second theme, and the cello brings in a third idea, a rising line of staccato triplets that echoes the opening motif. A brief development leads to a concise recapitulation and coda.

The "Prussian" Quartets (1789–1790)

In 1789 Mozart travelled to Potsdam with hopes of obtaining lucrative commissions from the music-loving Friedrich Wilhelm II of Prussia. While attending concerts at the palace, Mozart noted that Friedrich participated as a competent cellist in the programs. When Friedrich eventually commissioned several chamber works, Mozart decided to emphasize the king's own instrument—the cello. The resulting three "Prussian" Quartets build on the foundation that Mozart had established through close study of Haydn's string quartets, primarily his inventive Opus 33 (*Gli Scherzi*). However, Mozart's Prussian quartets expand the genre's lyrical potential because the cello is now showcased as a virtuoso instrument ranging melodically over three octaves rather than as a modest lower voice.

Severe problems with both health and finances beset Mozart after his return to Vienna. He suffered from headaches and insomnia, possibly because of Constanze's difficult fifth pregnancy as well as their desperate poverty. After sending several of the requested six quartets to the king and receiving a muted response, possibly because the virtuoso cello scores exceeded the king's abilities, Mozart sold his three completed Prussian Quartets to the publisher Artaria for ready cash—but without a dedication to Friedrich. Mozart wrote: "I have disposed of the quartets (all that toilsome work) for a mockery of a fee, only to keep myself going." Although the many erasures in the manuscripts indicate that the work possibly was "toilsome," the quartets develop with graceful elegance and lighthearted inventiveness.

String Quartet in D Major, K. 575 ("The Violet")

Allegretto
Andante
Menuetto: Allegretto
Allegretto

Mozart wrote his K. 575, the first of his "Prussian" Quartets, within a month of his return to Vienna in June 1789. The Allegro develops two buoyant themes, the first stated by the violin and the second—in a forte dynamic—by the cello. The lyrical and eloquent Andante (A major) is written in three-part song form. K. 575 has been nicknamed "The Violet" because the Andante's opening theme resembles Mozart's song *Das Veilchen*, his early setting of a Goethe poem.

The delightful Menuetto (D major) is animated by strong dynamic contrasts. Its trio section (G major) highlights the cello with a recurring ornamented phrase in its upper register. The main theme of the Allegretto finale, introduced by the cello, is a rising arpeggio that recalls the first theme of the opening Allegro. A rondo in form, the movement develops with brilliantly contrasting interludes and inventive counterpoint.

String Quartet in B flat Major, K. 589

Allegro
Larghetto
Menuetto: Moderato
Allegro assai

K. 589, the second "Prussian" Quartet, opens with a lyrical sonata form movement that develops four ideas. Although the first violin introduces the opening idea, the cello initiates the other themes, primarily in its songful upper register. After a brief development animated by vigorous triplet figures, a recapitulation expands on the opening ideas.

The Larghetto (E flat major) unfolds as a serene yet intense dialogue between the cello and the first violin. The cello's high opening phrase suggests an operatic aria; the violin offers a second idea, and the cello responds with a gracefully ornamented passage. At the conclusion thematic ideas dovetail among all four instruments, and the movement closes quietly.

The substantial Menuetto develops two energetic motifs with strong rhythmic profiles. The extensive three-part trio section (E flat major) begins and ends with a passage requiring vigorous string crossings for all instruments. At its center the violin plays passagework that appears improvised over accompanying figures in the other instruments. The Menuetto then returns for a literal repeat.

The unexpected pauses and sudden dynamic changes of the good-natured Allegro assai suggest the witty influence of Haydn's Opus 33 (*Gli Scherzi*) Quartets. Two ideas, the second of which is heard in the cello, are developed in sonata form. After a development notable for its harmonic excursions and subtle thematic dovetailing, the opening ideas are briefly recapitulated. The movement concludes with a quiet coda interrupted only by a single loud chord near its end.

String Quartet in F Major, K. 590

Allegro moderato
Allegretto
Menuetto: Allegretto
Allegro

Due to several false starts, Mozart's final string quartet, K. 590 (1790), was composed over a longer duration than his earlier quartets. Initially Mozart had projected a more simply constructed cello-centered work that would honor the King's instrument. Perhaps doubting the monarch's abilities as cellist, he abandoned that concept in favor of a string quartet with a new refinement—thematic material would be symmetrically distributed among the four voices to achieve unprecedented equality. This lofty goal required intense labor. Despite a variety of frustrations so immense that he chose to end his "Prussian" sequence with K. 590, the work develops with geniality and charm. The work is notable for both its good-natured themes and its high polish.

The quartet opens boldly with two motifs of utmost simplicity—a soft F major arpeggio and a loud, downward sweeping F major scale, both played unison by all four instruments. The first violin sculpts this material into a congenial theme, and the cello offers brief interjections. The cello introduces the second theme, which assumes greater prominence in the recapitulation. The coda offers a mirror image of the opening motifs, now extended to create a full dialogue.

The leisurely Allegretto (C major) begins with a stately motif played with unison rhythms by the four instruments. This central motif is enhanced by long, decorative lines heard in all voices. In the second section (E flat major) the cello enjoys extended virtuoso figuration that spans three octaves. A brief C major coda concludes the movement.

The Menuetto begins with an F major violin arpeggio that refers thematically to the opening movement. The cello introduces a second theme in the trio, which is animated by piquant (appoggiatura) ornamental notes at its conclusion.

The witty sonata rondo finale moves in nearly perpetual motion with successions of sixteenth notes. Sprightly ornamentation, an inventive fugal section, colorful harmonic excursions, and a suggestion of a bagpipe create a delightful farewell to Mozart's string quartet creation.

TRIOS WITH VARIED SCORING

Divertimento in E flat Major for Violin, Viola, and Cello, K. 563

Allegro
Adagio
Menuetto: Allegro; Trio
Andante
Menuetto: Allegretto; Trio I; Trio II
Allegro

Mozart's K. 563 Divertimento for String Trio, his only opus in this form, is recognized both as the greatest work written for the medium and as one of his finest chamber works. The masterful K. 563 was written during the phenomenally productive summer of 1788—during which Mozart created his three great symphonies in E flat, G minor, and C major ("Jupiter"). The term "divertimento" in the eighteenth century suggested an entertaining composition with a selection of simply constructed dancelike movements. However, Mozart's K. 563 projects symphonic scope and depth onto this popular form.

Mozart wrote K. 563 for his Masonic lodge brother Johann Michael von Puchberg, a Viennese merchant who generously loaned Mozart money during the final years of his life. With Mozart as violist, the work was performed first at the Dresden court—for which he received "a very handsome snuffbox"—and later at a private concert held in a Viennese palace.

The Allegro, written in sonata form, offers two cantabile themes that grow dark and restless in the development section. The charming mood of the opening returns at the recapitulation. The reflective Adagio, a sonata form movement in A flat major, continuously recasts its primary theme, a triadic figure heard at the outset in the cello.

The two menuetto movements differ in structure. The light-hearted first Menuetto is cast in traditional three-part form with a gentle trio intervening between its two primary statements. The lengthier second Menuetto suggests a rustic German dance. Two contrasting trio sections alternate with statements of the main theme, an idea that evokes hunting horns, and the movement concludes with a sprightly coda. Between these two Menuetti falls the significant Andante, a set of four continuous variations on a folklike theme. The beguiling Allegro finale develops its two themes in sonata rondo form, in which the principal themes are separated by contrasting episodes. A recurring drumbeat motif in all three instruments pushes the momentum and brings the work to an energetic conclusion.

Piano Trio in B flat Major, K. 502

Allegro
Larghetto
Allegretto

In his maturity Mozart wrote six piano trios, originally entitled "terzetten" to distinguish them from his earlier piano-dominated divertimenti trios. In K. 502 (1786), the third of the group and perhaps the most popular, all three instruments achieve independence; the violin enjoys an especially virtuosic part. Mozart indicated that the work was to be performed in "friendly, musical, social circles." Most probably this delightful work was written for the congenial family of Franziska von Jacquin, his talented piano student.

Unlike the majority of Mozart's sonata form chamber movements, which develop a variety of songlike themes, the Allegro is essentially monothematic. Derivations of the graceful opening idea are clearly heard in the second thematic area (F major) and in the concluding theme of the exposition. The development section introduces a new idea, but soon refocuses on the opening material.

The elegant Larghetto offers an intimate dialogue among the three instruments. The piano introduces the main ideas, which are answered and developed by the violin; the cello supports throughout. Lyrical interludes fall between statements of the opening theme.

The Allegretto opens with a gentle, dancelike motif in the piano, and the violin counters with a louder repeat. The cello and piano execute a repeated accompaniment figure as the violin plays a countersubject, an idea derived from the main theme. The two themes alternate throughout the remainder of this brilliant movement.

Piano Trio in E Major, K. 542

Allegro
Andante grazioso
Allegro

The summer of 1788 was an astoundingly productive time for Mozart, who wrote his final three symphonies, a piano sonata, and his esteemed K. 542 Piano Trio (the fourth of his six piano trios) within the space of three months. This period of heightened creativity coincided with particularly acute financial distress, resulting in a move to simpler lodgings, as well as emotional stress from the death of his six-month-old daughter Theresia. However, Mozart rarely allowed distressing external circumstances to deter his composition process.

Of the three piano trios written in 1788, K. 542 is considered the finest because of its fluidity and balance, as well as the haunting beauty that emerges from its deceptively simple materials. Mozart's trios of this period follow the same overall design—a sonata form movement in a fast tempo, a slower movement in a closely related key, and a rondo finale that begins with a piano statement. The piano introduces K. 542's twelve-measure opening theme, which is expanded by all three instruments. A transition leads to the second subject, also twelve measures long, and the exposition closes with a chromatic version of the opening theme; the material is developed fugally. The rondo form finale begins with a simple theme that evolves into an eloquent, harmonically rich statement in the strings.

Trio in E flat Major for Clarinet, Viola, and Piano, K. 498 ("Kegelstatt")

Andante
Menuetto
Allegretto

Mozart enjoyed the musical and social companionship of Anton Stadler, a formidable clarinet virtuoso who tirelessly experimented with new sonorities for his instrument. Stadler's enthusiasm was contagious for Mozart, and he willingly created both orchestral passages and chamber works to showcase Stadler's artistry. In addition to musical collaborations, the good-natured Stadler frequently joined Mozart for games of billiards and skittles.

K. 498 is nicknamed the "Kegelstatt," or the "Bowling Alley" Trio, for the most probable reason that Mozart composed this luminous work while bowling with Stadler. Mozart had been asked to compose a work for his pupil Franziska von Jacquin, daughter of a music-loving Viennese family who frequently entertained Mozart at their home. The story goes that Mozart remembered this assignment while bowling. In between sets he wrote his poetic K. 498 for Stadler on clarinet, himself on viola, and Franziska on piano.

Essentially monothematic, the Andante develops a lyrical theme characterized by a rapid ornamental turn. Interplay among the three instrumental lines reveals subtle blends and contrasts of sonority. Propelled by an emphatic bass line, the Menuetto achieves drama through abrupt changes of dynamics. The contrasting trio section develops a dialogue between the clarinet and viola. The Menuetto returns and the movement closes with an echo of the trio ideas.

The Allegretto is a rondo with an A-B-A-C-A-D-A structure. Each A section is a repetition of the principal theme and the other sections offer contrasting interludes. Animated by elegant counterpoint and energetic arpeggiated figures, the finale moves to a radiant conclusion.

QUARTETS WITH VARIED SCORING

Quartet in D Major for Flute and Strings, K. 285

Allegro
Adagio
Rondeau

In 1777 Mozart grew restless due to lack of opportunity in his native Salzburg. He resigned from his court position with his unappreciative employer, Prince Archbishop Hieronymus Colloredo, and embarked on a tour to seek a more favorable post. Although unsuccessful, Mozart did receive enough commissions along the way to finance his travels. One welcome patron was Ferdinand Dejean, a surgeon in the Dutch East India Company and an accomplished amateur flutist. Dejean offered 200 guilders for "three small, easy, brief flute concertos and several flute quartets." Mozart undertook the commission with enthusiasm, but his interest was soon diverted by other projects; nevertheless, he managed to complete two flute concertos and three flute quartets. Dejean judged the resulting compositions to be of uneven quality and, to Mozart's chagrin, paid only half the agreed fee.

Mozart completed K. 285 in Mannheim on Christmas Day, 1779. A delightful miniature, it has retained a popular position in the flute ensemble repertoire. The opening Allegro develops two songful themes in an uncomplicated Rococo style. The Adagio is a graceful serenade for flute accompanied by pizzicati in the strings. A graceful theme alternates with contrasting episodes in the spirited Rondeau finale.

Quartet in F Major for Oboe and Strings, K. 370

Allegro
Adagio
Rondeau: Allegro

In 1780 the Elector of Bavaria invited Mozart to Munich to compose an opera to be performed during the upcoming carnival season. Mozart's employer in Salzburg, Prince Archbishop Hieronymous Colloredo, reluctantly granted him leave for six weeks, but Mozart managed to gain a four-month extension to complete and rehearse *Idomeneo*, his first significant serious opera. During this time Mozart renewed his friendship with Friedrich Ramm, the principal oboist of the Elector's orchestra. Mozart had heard Ramm's exquisite playing four years earlier and had then resolved to create a work showcasing Ramm's considerable abilities. Immediately after composing his opera, Mozart began his K. 370 Oboe Quartet and completed it early in 1781.

When Mozart combined string instruments with winds in his chamber works, he invariably replaced the first violin line with the wind instrument—which easily dominates the group because of its stronger tonal color. To achieve his desired homogeneity of sound, as well as the conversational qualities of chamber music, in

K. 370 Mozart integrates all four voices through subtle dovetailing of melody and countermelody. Nevertheless, the oboe line is always prominent in K. 370, a testimony to its conception as a showpiece for his friend's virtuosity.

The Allegro opens with a lively theme stated by the oboe. The violin plays the elegant rococo second theme, closely related to the first motif, as the oboe articulates a countermelody. After a development featuring virtuoso passagework for each performer and a recapitulation of the first theme, the movement concludes with a quiet coda.

The Adagio (D minor), a brief but concentrated 38 measures long, is a sustained, expressive aria for oboe. The delightful Rondeau finale offers virtuoso passages for the oboist; in a remarkable central episode the oboe climbs dramatically to its highest register before the strings reprise the main theme. The work concludes with three ascending notes that echo the closing of the Adagio.

Piano Quartet in G Minor, K. 478

Allegro
Andante
Rondo (Allegro)

In 1785 Mozart contracted with his friend and publisher Franz Anton Hoffmeister to write three piano quartets, a new genre that promised to be marketable to the many Viennese amateur pianists. At that time the piano was not a full thematic partner in the ensemble; early chamber works most often used the keyboard to fill out harmonies supporting the string lines. K. 478, the first of the two piano quartets that Mozart completed, is a breakthrough work in which the piano and the string group achieve equality. The piano score, so virtuoso that it on occasion resembles a concerto, is balanced by equally strong string lines to create a unified chamber work.

Unfortunately for Mozart, Hoffmeister assessed K. 478 as being too difficult for his clients, and he declined to publish it—but he did allow the cash-strapped Mozart to keep the money that had been advanced. However, Mozart wrote a second piano quartet a few months later and sought out a new venue—Artaria, who became his primary publisher.

K. 478 is cast in G minor, a dark key that Mozart favored for his more turbulent works. The terse opening theme, played in unison by all instruments, solidifies this tonality; the solo piano responds with an extension to the phrase, which is then repeated and developed by all instruments. The piano introduces a calmer second subject (B flat major) first developed contrapuntally by the strings then recast with varied rhythms. The piano states a third theme, echoed by the violin. After a brief but dramatic development, the themes undergo further development in the recapitulation. The emphatic coda reiterates the succinct opening motive.

The Andante (B flat major), in sonata form, develops two expressive melodies, both stated first in the piano. Colorful recasts of scoring enhance the fervency of these lyrical themes. The rondo finale (G major) opens with a buoyant idea in the piano; an energetic theme follows in the strings. The brilliant piano score demands virtuosity throughout.

QUINTETS WITH VARIED SCORING

Mozart's string quintets are also known as viola quintets—string quartets with an additional viola. This sonorous instrumentation appealed to Mozart, who frequently played viola in chamber ensembles, and over the course of his career he composed six of these quintets. Compared to his string quartets, Mozart's viola quintets reveal richer harmonies and a freer exchange of thematic material. For Mozart, the extra middle voice inspired inventive musical dialogue. Many listeners believe that Mozart's set of viola quintets constitutes his most profound achievement in chamber music.

String Quintet in B flat Major, K. 174

Allegro moderato
Adagio
Menuetto ma allegretto
Allegro

Mozart was introduced to the viola quintet form by his friend Michael Haydn, Joseph's brother. Michael had completed his first viola quintet in February 1773, and the seventeen-year-old Mozart was sufficiently impressed to work on his own quintet for an uncharacteristic length of three months. Mozart's first effort resembled Michael's quintet in its sequence of movements, prominence of the first violin and first viola, frequent echo effects, and codas at the ends of the movements. However, by December Michael had completed a second viola quintet, and Mozart was stunned by his friend's improvement. He quickly recast the last two movements of K. 174 with more elaborate counterpoint and longer sections of development. Although pleased with his new version, fourteen years passed before he attempted another viola quintet.

The delightful Allegro moderato unfolds in sonata form—after full statements of the themes, a development section follows with several harmonic surprises, then the opening material clearly returns. The expressive center of K. 174, the songful Adagio (E flat major) features exchanges between the first violin and first viola. The Menuetto, which resembles a rustic dance, is varied by the smoother trio section at its center. The finale develops with interesting dialogues and echo effects among the instruments.

String Quintet in G Minor, K. 516

Allegro
Menuetto: Allegretto
Adagio, ma non troppo
Adagio—Allegro

The key of G minor has been described as "the key of fate" for Mozart since many of his most powerful and portentous works—such as his Symphony No. 40—have been set in that key. The somber G minor modality pervades the entire quintet. At the opening of the Allegro the violin initiates the "fate" theme constructed from two brief and simple motifs—a rising G minor arpeggio and a descending G minor chromatic scale fragment. The first viola responds with a related theme in G minor to ground the tonality. The restless Menuetto, also in G minor, grows unsettled through punctuations of loudly accented chords on unexpected beats; a gentle trio section (G major) unfolds with falling intervals separated by rests that suggest sighs. The atmosphere remains subdued as the mode shifts to E flat major in the muted Adagio, ma non troppo, a poignant dialogue between the first viola and cello. Tchaikovsky wrote to his patroness Madame von Meck: "No one has ever with such beauty expressed in music the feeling of resigned, helpless grief."

The following G minor Adagio, only 38 measures long, is a profound lament; the simplicity of its pizzicato cello accompaniment underscores the atmosphere of inward sorrow. The final Allegro, a joyful rondo in G major, proceeds without pause. The exuberance of this rondo has created controversy among listeners. Some hear the Allegro as a trivial irrelevance to the gravity that precedes; others suggest a dramatic function—perhaps a happy resolution to a troubled operatic scene. Because a G minor fragment to this movement exists, it is probable that Mozart at least considered other possibilities for the quintet's conclusion.

Quintet in E flat Major for Horn and Strings, K. 407

Allegro
Andante
Rondo: Allegro

During his adolescence whenever Mozart wished to play his notorious practical jokes or exchange ribald stories, he sought out Ignaz Leutgeb, a French horn player in the Salzburg orchestra. Mozart and Leutgeb were such kindred spirits that when Mozart moved to Vienna the hornist followed him. There Leutgeb opened a cheese shop with the financial assistance of Mozart's father. Despite his flourishing business, Leutgeb continued to perform his French horn, then a valveless instrument that had only recently been adapted from the hunting horn. Since little concert literature existed for this difficult new instrument, which both composers and audiences then considered somewhat unrefined, Mozart wrote four horn concertos and the K. 407 Quintet. The quintet's manuscript, which was completed in December 1782, contains numerous observations for Leutgeb: "Go to it, Signor Donkey"—"Take a little breath"—"Thank God, here's the end."

Because of its extraordinarily demanding horn part, the quintet often resembles a concerto with the unusual chamber accompaniment of violin, two violas, and cello. The vigorous opening Allegro explores contrasts of tonal qualities between the horn and strings as it develops two contrasting themes in sonata form. The closest rapport between the instruments occurs in the Andante, a serene movement in which all five instruments contribute to the development of the principal theme. The high-spirited rondo finale opens with rhythmic ambiguities that obscure the principal theme's beginning. Does the idea begin on the upbeat or the downbeat? Here is a musical joke aimed at Leutgeb.

Quintet in E flat Major for Piano and Winds, K. 452

Largo—Allegro moderato
Larghetto
Allegretto

Mozart completed K. 452, his only quintet for piano and winds, two days before its scheduled premiere in April, 1784. He wrote to his father Leopold: "I composed a quintet which called forth the greatest applause. I consider it to be the best work I have ever composed." Mozart set a difficult goal for himself with the quintet's unusual instrumentation. He understood the challenge of achieving an elegant blend of voices with single instruments rather than those in pairs, but he compensated for the diverse timbres through the utmost subtlety of phrasing and scoring. The first piano and woodwind quintet ever published, K. 452 is an ingenious work of refined expression. It was especially admired by Beethoven, who wrote his similarly scored Opus 16 Piano Quintet as homage.

At the time he wrote the quintet, Mozart was also composing his first set of mature string quartets. He conceived these six quartets, famously dedicated to Joseph Haydn ("from whom I have learned to write quartets"), as discourses among all instruments rather than as individual showpieces. A similar esthetic prevails in K. 452, for throughout the quintet all instruments share the development of ideas, which are generally introduced by the piano.

The masterfully crafted Allegro moderato, in sonata form, develops its long phrases through short motivic contributions from the various instruments, each prominent only briefly. In the sublime Larghetto (B flat major), written in the style of an operatic aria, the two sustained themes develop through subtle interweaving of the five instrumental parts. At the end of the rondo finale each instrument participates in the brilliant ensemble cadenza, normally a tour de force for the individual soloist.

Quintet in A Major for Clarinet and Strings, K. 581

Allegro
Larghetto
Menuetto
Allegretto con variazioni

Mozart called his K. 581 Clarinet Quintet (1789) the "Stadler Quintet" in honor of his virtuoso clarinetist friend, Anton Stadler. Stadler, a careless spender who kept a mistress, was not regarded as one of Vienna's finer citizens, but he was respected as one of its finest musicians. He contributed to the development of the clarinet by promoting extensions of its lower register, and he enhanced its repertoire through his collaborations with Mozart, who also wrote his clarinet concerto for him. Aside from their musical association, Mozart thoroughly enjoyed his company, despite Stadler's occasionally outrageous exploitation of his generosity.

The Allegro develops a glorious succession of singing melodies. In the first theme group alone, three distinct melodies are joined to form a graceful arc. After a brief pause the violin presents the second theme, which is soon followed by a lyrical third idea shared by the clarinet and violin. The second movement (D major) is an extended song for clarinet accompanied by the muted strings. The third movement, the expressive Menuetto, departs from tradition in that it contains two trios rather than the customary single trio— first, a mysterious statement for strings in the minor mode and second, a rustic dance that features the clarinet. The final Allegretto is a set of six buoyant variations that suggest German folk music.

THREE

A Genre Evolves:
Beethoven's Piano Trios

LUDWIG VAN BEETHOVEN
B. DECEMBER 16, 1770 IN BONN,
D. MARCH 26, 1827 IN VIENNA

Beethoven launched his career with his piano trios. Originally better known as a pianist than as a composer, he began to create these trios for his own performances during his early years in Bonn. Then a relatively new genre, the piano trio had gained popularity in the middle of the eighteenth century after the hammer action of the pianoforte (or variously fortepiano) had been perfected. With this mechanism the player could achieve an even tone and a variety of dynamic shadings, and the piano became a welcome member of the chamber ensemble.

Beethoven anticipated curious audiences for piano trios as well as minimal competition from established composers, a wise evaluation for an emerging one. The piano trio for both Mozart and Haydn had been of less interest than the symphony or string quartet. Mozart, now deceased, had limited his production to six. Although Haydn was a pioneer of the form, the majority of his piano trios can be heard as keyboard-centered works with the cello scored to reinforce the weak lower register of his thinly-strung piano and the violin scored to complement his piano's silvery upper range. (Haydn considered the more fully-voiced pianos of his day to be unreliable and too expensive.) Beethoven revolutionized the form with his twelve bold and sonorous piano trios, nine of which were published during his lifetime. These grandly scaled and finely nuanced works reveal his stylistic evolution up until the final stage of his career, when he ceased to perform because of his deafness.

Piano Trio in E flat Major (Fourteen Variations on an Original Theme), Opus 44

Beethoven wrote his Opus 44 Variations during his final year of apprenticeship in Bonn, a time when he experimented productively with piano trio ideas, many in the "noble" key of E flat major. The great pioneer music researcher Gustav Nottebohm, who discovered a sketch of these variations next to a draft for the catalogued song *Feuerfarbe*, pinpoints their composition date at 1792. However, Beethoven kept the variations hidden among his personal papers for twelve years. He finally chose to publish the variations outside his resident city of Vienna, and in 1804 he offered them to the Leipzig firm of Hoffmeister with a letter nearly apologetic in tone. Although these elegant variations do not compare in stature to the great works that followed in the piano trio genre, they constitute a charming set that is close in spirit to the Rococo style of the earlier eighteenth century.

Beethoven crafted a symmetrical and strongly tonal theme as the basis for his fourteen variations. Introduced as a staccato statement by all three instruments, the theme is enhanced first by florid passagework in the piano and then is developed gracefully by the other instruments. Strong contrasts of dynamics, rhythm, register, and pianistic texture animate the set. The minor key variations, numbers VII and XII, are notable for their expressive lyricism.

THE OPUS 1 TRIOS (1791–1794)

A composer's Opus 1 marks the critical transition from apprentice status to that of a professional prepared to bear public scrutiny. Beethoven, always a perfectionist, had followed a long apprenticeship. He had completed nineteen chamber works during his early years in Bonn, a sociable court city eager to hear works in progress—including selections from his Opus 1 set as it evolved. In 1792 he relocated to Vienna, where he sought a mentor as he continued work on his three Opus 1 Trios. His idol then was Mozart, whom he had met briefly during an early visit to Vienna, and he planned to study with him once he relocated there. After Mozart's early death devastated these hopes, Beethoven engaged Joseph Haydn, now retired to Vienna from the Esterházy estates. Several composition sessions were held in Viennese coffee houses, and Beethoven willingly paid for both the instruction and the coffees. However, Beethoven proved to be an unreceptive student for the aging Haydn, whose main fault for "The Great Mogul" (Haydn's term for Beethoven) was that he was not Mozart. Although Beethoven resisted Haydn's instructional guidance, he respected the master's compositions. As Mozart did in the past, Beethoven closely examined Haydn's scores to absorb his techniques. He also studied Mozart's chamber music scores—as did Haydn, who recognized Mozart's genius and had the humility to learn from him at a late stage of his career.

Formally based on classical principles, the Opus 1 Trios reveal stylistic affinities to Mozart's "Haydn" Quartets (works dedicated to the older master), which Beethoven would have studied and performed as a string player. Both composers follow Haydn's process of "thematic elaboration" to achieve supple forms that develop organically through the growth of short motifs heard at the beginnings of movements. Yet the expanded dynamic range of Beethoven's trios is strikingly new, especially the sudden changes from very soft to very loud. The trios also offer hints of Beethoven's proto-Romantic tendency to allow a movement's poetic flow to shape its formal development.

A year after his arrival, established as a pianist and befriended by several nobles, Beethoven presented the premiere performance of all three trios at the home of Prince Karl Lichnowsky. The musical elite of Vienna, including Haydn, was present. Stung by criticism from Haydn, who expressed approval for all but the third trio of the set, Beethoven continued to work on Opus 1 for another year before submitting it for publication—an event eagerly greeted by Vienna's many amateur piano trio performers, who had long known of these works through word of mouth.

Piano Trio in E flat Major, Opus 1 No. 1

Allegro
Adagio cantabile
Scherzo: Allegro assai
Finale: Presto

Beethoven composed his three Opus 1 Trios with their specific order firmly in mind. It is perhaps beyond coincidence that the key centers of each trio (E flat, G, and C) together form the chord of C minor, his signature tonality throughout his career. Opus 1 No. 1 (E flat major) would then constitute the fulcrum of the set; the other two trios form a pairing that gravitates toward C minor. Most certainly the key of E flat was an appropriate choice for the first trio. The bright E flat tonality was understood to convey majesty and heroism—congenial affects for Beethoven's courtly audience.

The E flat Trio opens with an energetic, upward-moving arpeggiated figure known as the "Mannheim rocket," a brilliant effect used by composers associated with the Mannheim court in the mid-eighteenth century; this gesture in varying guises pervades all four movements of the trio. A gentle second subject is introduced in rhythmic unison by all instruments, and both ideas are developed in sonata form. The movement closes with a coda far more extensive than had been heard in works of his predecessors, an indication that Beethoven was reevaluating classical balances.

The Adagio cantabile (A flat major) begins with a light and songful piano theme that gradually achieves profundity. Structured as a rondo, the movement offers three slightly varied thematic statements separated by interludes of increasing poignancy. Darkly expressive harmonic realms haunt its center.

The dancelike Scherzo unfolds in A-B-A form with ingratiating themes animated by grace notes. In the central trio section (A flat major), the strings play sustained lines as the piano softly echoes Mannheim rocket figures. The movement ends quietly with a brief coda.

The vivacious Finale, in sonata form, opens with a large leap in the piano followed by a descending arpeggio; the violin introduces a contrasting second theme. Both themes are developed in sonata form but are recast with new freedom at the recapitulation. The strings echo the rocket theme at the energetic coda.

Piano Trio in G Major, Opus 1 No. 2

Adagio—Allegro vivace
Largo con espressione
Scherzo: Allegro
Finale: Presto

At the time Beethoven wrote his G Major Trio he closely studied Mozart's scores together with Haydn's chamber works. Opus 1 No. 2 reveals affinities of both style and key to Mozart's K. 387 string quartet, which Beethoven admired so strongly that he wrote out a full copy of its score to better absorb its techniques.

Beethoven was sensitive to the specific sounds of individual keys, a perception enhanced by eighteenth-century tuning systems that yielded differing overtones within the scales. Equal temperament was then in vogue but the consonant intonation of meantone tuning had its advocates (especially string players and organists.) G major in his day was described as a "pure" key, well in tune on the keyboard ideally adjusted to meantone. A versatile tonality, it was considered suitable for lighthearted works that included more serious statements—a reasonable choice for the essentially good-natured Opus 1 No. 2.

The substantial Adagio introduction opens with two gestures that establish the tonality—a forceful G major chord followed by a soft G major arpeggio. The piano previews the Allegro's first theme; hints of themes to come are woven throughout the piano score and string lines. A rising piano scale leads directly to the Allegro, which develops two ideas in sonata form. Motivic exchanges between the strings and piano recall Haydn's whimsical humor. Themes move through remote harmonies in the compact development; in the recapitulation ideas are expanded through inventive piano passagework and extensive string duets that exchange motivic fragments imitatively. The brief coda reiterates the arpeggios heard at the opening measures.

The reflective three-part Largo (E major) develops with nuanced lyricism that suggests the influence of Mozart. All instruments share extended passages of glorious song. Richly colorful harmonies underpin the free thematic development, especially poignant in the minor mode passages. The E major tonality is reestablished at the hushed conclusion.

The solo cello introduces the Scherzo (G major) in its lowest register, and the other instruments answer imitatively. The second phrase extends this theme, now punctuated with unexpected accents. The contrasting trio (B minor) begins quietly with a lightly accompanied piano statement. The cello introduces a new theme, a staccato passage accompanied by trills in the piano's upper register. The opening Scherzo is repeated, and the movement concludes with a coda that softly reiterates the Scherzo's main theme.

The Presto finale is a virtuoso tour de force for the piano. Cast in sonata form, this ebullient movement develops two contrasting themes—the first rapid and propulsive, the second a calmer suggestion of the opening movement's first theme. The development recasts both themes in new key areas. The buoyant recapitulation unfolds with inventive detail, and the movement concludes with a fortissimo statement of its opening theme.

Piano Trio in C Minor, Opus 1 No. 3

Allegro con brio
Andante cantabile con variazioni
Menuetto: Quasi Allegro
Finale: Prestissimo

Beethoven found his own voice in the Opus 1 No. 3 Trio, his first work in the significant key of C minor—for him the implacable "key of Fate." He considered this bold trio to be the finest of the three and the most original. He was therefore stunned when his mentor Haydn suggested that he not publish this trio "because the public would not understand it." After making certain alterations, Beethoven nevertheless published the trio together with the other two of the set—but the dedication of the work to Prince Lichnowsky made no mention of his mentor, who had hoped that "Pupil of Haydn" would be inscribed on the cover.

The Allegro opens with a soft but terse motivic statement played in unison by all three instruments; the piano then extends the theme into a lilting melody. The cello introduces a second subject, again expanded by all three instruments. The compact development recasts both themes with new harmonies; emphatic descending piano scales (G major) prepare the return of the C minor opening theme, now heard in a fortissimo dynamic. A brief Adagio passage slows the momentum, then the opening theme returns softly. Beethoven now surprises the listener by appearing to back away from the ending—which arrives with a forceful cascade of piano scales and off-beat accents.

The Andante cantabile (E flat major) offers five variations of a serene melody and a summarizing coda. At the first variation the piano, lightly accompanied by the strings, ornaments the theme with graceful turns. The cello initiates a duet with violin in the second variation; the piano provides complementary thematic support. In Variation III the piano assumes leadership; pizzicato lines in the strings add urgency to the furious piano score. The cello leads the string duet in the poignant Variation IV (E flat minor). Variation V, marked "a little slower," returns to the major mode with virtuoso staccato passagework in the piano. The opening tempo returns at the coda, and the movement concludes quietly.

The Menuetto (C minor) is an intense, driving movement that is punctuated by emphatic off beat accents and fortissimo chords. Its central trio section (C major) provides a gentle contrast. The Prestissimo finale (C minor), in sonata form, develops two contrasting themes that are stated at the outset—the first, an explosive piano figure, is a classic "Mannheim rocket," and the second is a calmer idea in E flat major. After a brief development with much virtuoso piano passagework, the keyboard leads to a return of the opening material. Ascending piano scales at the brief coda bring the work to a soft conclusion in C major.

Trio for Clarinet, Cello, and Piano in B flat Major, Opus 11 ("Gassenhauer")

Allegro con brio
Adagio
Tema con variazioni: Allegretto

Classical era composers valued the clarinet as an important asset to orchestral scoring, but only rarely did they create chamber literature for the instrument. Beethoven composed his Opus 11

Trio as a favor to his clarinetist friend, the Czech virtuoso Joseph Beer. He honored Beer's request to include a variation movement based on a tune from a then-fashionable opera, Joseph Weigl's *L'amor marinaro*. Written early in Beethoven's career (1796, published in 1798), the trio reveals its eighteenth-century roots in its three-movement format (fast-slow-fast), its motivic development in the manner of Haydn, and its clearly phrased melodic lines animated by complementary contrapuntal material. The full piano texture suggests the influence of the brilliant pianist (and innovative composer) Muzio Clementi. Beethoven himself rescored the work for the more standard trio instrumentation of violin, cello, and piano to increase sales; the violin line closely follows the original clarinet part.

The opening movement is an expansive Allegro that unfolds in classical sonata form. The Adagio is based on a songful theme presented first by the cello then embellished by the other instruments. The finale is a set of nine variations on *L'amor marinaro*'s popular theme *Pria ch'io l'impegno* ("Before I Made That Promise"). The theme reappears in new guises to conjure contrasting moods.

THE OPUS 70 TRIOS (1808)

Within a few years after arriving in Vienna, Beethoven was celebrated as Europe's greatest pianist, its greatest composer of piano works, and a symphonist on a par with Haydn. He enjoyed the friendship and patronage of numerous aristocrats and fruitful relationships with his publishers. However, his growing deafness was a source of deep anguish. In 1802 he wrote a letter to his brothers from the town of Heiligenstadt: "I fear that I may be subjected to the danger of letting my condition be observed... I have been at the verge of despair, and but little more and I would put an end to my life. Only art it was that withheld me—it seemed impossible to leave the world until I had produced all I felt called upon to produce." Despite this misfortune, Beethoven continued to compose works that reflected moods both good-natured and serene. He embarked on a productive "middle period," roughly extending from 1803 to 1809, and created numerous large-scale compositions notable for their fluent technique and subtle originality.

Beethoven wrote his two Opus 70 Trios in 1808, the same year he composed his masterful "Emperor" Piano Concerto. During this period, he roomed at the palace of Maria Erdődy, a deceptively fragile widow whose friendship had sustained him when he first recognized his increasing deafness. He dedicated both Opus 70 Trios to Maria, whom he affectionately called his "Father Confessor," and held both premieres at her salon.

Piano Trio in D Major, Opus 70 No. 1 ("Ghost")

Allegro vivace e con brio
Largo assai ed espressivo
Presto

Opus 70 No. 1 opens with a statement of two motifs—an assertive figure played in unison by all three instruments, followed by a singing cello phrase that is immediately echoed by the violin and piano. The piano then introduces an emphatic third motif, accompanied by scale passages in the strings. After a succinct development, the recapitulation expands the opening ideas.

Listeners, not Beethoven, have named Opus 70 No. 1 "The Ghost" because of its eerie Largo assai, a complete and dramatic contrast to the extroverted opening movement. Partially based on sketches for the witches' scene from his projected opera *Macbeth*, this somber D minor movement sustains an atmosphere of mystery and foreboding. Ominous crescendos and diminuendos underpin the two plaintive motives that recur throughout. Darkly shimmering figuration in the piano provides a suspenseful transition to the vigorous Presto (D major), which proceeds without pause. Clearly structured in classical sonata form and animated by playful passages of imitation among all instruments, this rapid movement provides warm relief from the stark and uncertain atmosphere of the Largo. Its two ideas, both of which reference thematic notes of the Largo, develop with genial expansiveness. A spirited coda concludes the movement.

Piano Trio in E flat Major, Opus 70 No. 2

Poco sostenuto: Allegro ma non troppo
Allegretto
Allegretto ma non troppo
Finale: Allegro

The genial Opus 70 No. 2 is often described as a model of trio construction because of its perfect balance among the three instruments. Perhaps inspired by the virtuoso playing of cellist Joseph Linke, who also roomed at the palace of Countess Erdődy, Beethoven fully emancipates this versatile instrument from its customary supporting role and allows it to sing thematic lines. The piano score is often set in a different register from the strings, allowing them to be heard as distinct thematic units.

The introduction to Opus 70 No. 2 begins with a serenely flowing melody initiated by the cello and expanded imitatively by the other instruments. In the Allegro section, three motifs are developed in sonata form. After a development with varied scoring and unexpected harmonic excursions, the opening ideas are recapitulated. In the coda, the introduction's amiable theme returns as a reprise.

A set of double variations, the Allegretto explores two contrasting ideas—a quietly flowing theme and a stridently martial idea. The two themes are expanded in alternating C major and C minor sections.

The Allegretto ma non troppo (A flat major) is structured as an elegant scherzo with two thematic ideas alternating in a five-part structure (A-B-A-B-A); its conclusion projects quiet introspection. The brilliant finale (E flat major) develops three subjects in classical sonata form and concludes with an expansive coda.

Piano Trio in B flat Major, Opus 97 ("Archduke")

Allegro moderato
Scherzo: Allegro
Andante cantabile, ma però con moto
Allegro moderato

Beethoven composed his Opus 97 Piano Trio in March 1811 and dedicated it to his piano student and patron, the Archduke Rudolph, younger brother of the Emperor of Austria. Beethoven himself performed the piano part at the work's premiere, held in April 1814 for a charity benefit. Because of his increasing deafness, this was to be Beethoven's last public appearance as a pianist. Fellow composer Ludwig Spohr sadly described the performance: "In forte passages, the poor deaf man pounded on the keys until the strings jangled, and in the piano sections he played so softly that whole groups of notes were omitted." The last of his piano trios, the "Archduke" is considered to be his greatest work in this medium.

Like most of his chamber works of his middle period, the trio begins with a movement in sonata form—a framework established by earlier classicists that organizes ideas into a coherent succession: an exposition of motifs, followed by a development of these ideas; then a recapitulation related to the opening section and a concluding coda. Within this scheme, Beethoven achieved maximum dramatic expression through contrasting modulations, particularly in the development section, and his uniquely flexible treatment of themes.

The Allegro moderato opens with a broad theme (B flat major) that establishes the expansive mood of the entire work. A gently descending second subject (G major) is heard first in the piano and then assumed by the strings. The development section is a sustained conversation among all three instruments as they explore elements of the exposition's opening themes. After a restatement of ideas, the movement concludes with a brief coda.

A vivacious tune in the strings opens the Scherzo, which alternates twice with the two-part Trio—a substantial section that consists of a mysterious fugato and a contrasting dance.

The Andante cantabile (marked "slow and singing, however with motion") offers five variations and a recitative coda on a hymnlike theme. In each variation the melody undergoes a radical transformation, but its harmonic structure is largely maintained.

The sublime mood is disrupted by the energetic rondo finale, which follows without pause. Virtuoso piano writing is heard throughout this brilliant movement, in which four appearances of the main theme alternate with contrasting episodes that refer thematically to earlier ideas. Near its end a change of meter from 2/4 to 6/8 accelerates the momentum, driving the work to an exhilarating conclusion.

Variations in G Major on "Ich bin der Schneider Kakadu," Opus 121a

The final piano trio published during Beethoven's lifetime, the set of ten charming variations on the theme *Ich bin der Schneider Kakadu* ("I Am the Tailor Kakadu," 1824), was most probably written twenty years earlier. Beethoven borrowed the theme from a fashionable light opera, *The Sisters of Prague* (1794) by Wenzel Müller, a prolific composer immensely popular in Vienna.

The Adagio introduction in G minor, made portentous by its persistent chromaticism, precedes the first statement of the theme—a clearly-cut tune in G major. Each instrument takes its separate turn in the opening variations: the solo piano performs the first, the violin takes the second, and the cello enjoys the solo line in the third. After these introductions, the score alternates between moments of technical display—such as the piano tour de force of Variation VI—and moments of melodious invention, as Variation VII's graceful duet for violin and cello. Variation IX, Adagio espressivo, returns to the poignant G minor theme of the opening. The brilliant finale begins with a light and rapid section that shifts from G major to G minor. The theme is repeated nearly in its original form, and the work concludes with a display of pianistic virtuosity.

FOUR

The Touchstone:
Beethoven's String Quartets

LUDWIG VAN BEETHOVEN
B. DECEMBER 16, 1770 IN BONN,
D. MARCH 26, 1827 IN VIENNA

Beethoven held the string quartet genre in his highest esteem. The sixteen that he composed over the course of his career are considered to be the most profound expressions of his inner thoughts; they are also judged to be the finest achievements in the genre. The traditions of Classicism passed to Beethoven through Mozart and Haydn and remained his ideals—he retained not only Classicism's concept of balance and proportion but also its high standard of craftsmanship. While Beethoven did acknowledge the virtue of inspiration, with the utmost rationality he continuously polished and improved his works, which he once described as "products of the human brain."

However, the influence of new cultural forces was immense. A broadly European reaction to rational materialism had launched the Romantic movement near the time of Beethoven's birth. Especially during the middle and late stages of his career, his compositions began to reflect traits associated with musical Romanticism—literary or descriptive programs (as in the middle quartets); a freer flow of thematically connected movements (as heard in the late quartets); a wide and subtle range of dynamics (heard in all quartets). Perhaps of equal importance, his personal concept was that of the Romantic artist, one who belonged to the highest level of humanity. As he remarked to an early patron, Prince Lichnowsky: "There are and will be thousands of princes. There is only one Beethoven."

EARLY QUARTETS (1798–1800)

Before Beethoven left Bonn for Vienna in 1792, his friend Count Waldstein told him that there "he would receive the spirit of Mozart from Haydn's hands." Beethoven had hoped to study with Mozart in Vienna—but since Mozart had recently died, Beethoven undertook instruction from Haydn instead. However, Beethoven, whom Haydn called "The Great Mogul," was too impatient to appreciate the master's lessons, and the studies soon ended because of their temperamental differences. But when Beethoven began to write his Opus 18 Quartets in 1798, he closely examined the mature quartets of Mozart and especially Haydn for guiding principles. A high point of his "first style period," the Opus 18 set reveals the pervasive influence of Haydn and Mozart but hints at the imminent expansion of Classicism's boundaries. Beethoven's originality is evident in all six Opus 18 Quartets, each of which opens with a small generative idea that gradually expands to form a large and uniquely detailed design.

Despite Haydn's position as Beethoven's early mentor, it was reported that when the aging composer heard these inventive and deeply expressive quartets at Prince Lobkowitz's concerts, he decided to abandon string quartets and devote his efforts to choral masses. Since Viennese composers typically avoided competing genres, this observation most probably holds truth.

String Quartet in F Major, Opus 18 No. 1

Allegro con brio
Adagio affettuoso ed appassionato
Scherzo: Allegro molto
Allegro

Although Beethoven's sketchbooks indicate that Opus 18 No. 1 was the second of the set to be written, he placed it first for publication because he favored its subtle inventiveness. He was annoyed that Nos. 2 and 4 received greater favor and was moved to profanity by a critical review of No. 1 in Vienna's leading music journal: "It is difficult to perform and not at all popular."

The Allegro con brio opens with a concise idea played in unison by all the strings. A second theme is introduced by the first violin; as in the quartets of Haydn, these two generative ideas expand to create a large and coherent design. The concluding coda introduces a scalar motive that combines with earlier ideas.

Beethoven's affinity with the growing Romantic movement is heard in the profound and intense Adagio (D minor), which develops three expressive themes. According to Beethoven's friend Karl Amenda, this movement was inspired by the tomb scene from Shakespeare's *Romeo and Juliet*. Beethoven penned the words *Les derniers soupirs* ("The final sighs") over the original end of the movement in his sketchbook.

The Scherzo movement (F major) unfolds with Mozartean grace. Robust octave exchanges introduce the flowing trio section; a repeat of the opening material follows. The Allegro finale, written in sonata rondo form, recalls the spirited finales of Haydn's quartets. It opens with a witty, rapid figure played in turn by each instrument. Contrasting episodes enter between the virtuoso thematic statements.

String Quartet in G Major, Opus 18 No. 2

Allegro
Adagio cantabile
Scherzo: Allegro
Allegro molto, quasi presto

The G Major Quartet (1798) conjures a graceful mood that is close in spirit to the Rococo style of the earlier eighteenth century. Its subtitle "Compliments" was bestowed a century after its composition by a critic who heard in its elegant opening phrases the suggestion of "an eighteenth-century salon, with all the ceremonious display and flourish of courtesy typical of the period—bows and gracious words of greeting."

Although this tightly unified quartet appears to have been effortlessly composed, Beethoven's sketchbooks reveal the intensive labor of its creation. His thirty-two pages of drafts demonstrate that the quartet began as many disparate elements that only gradually merged into a coherent whole. Strongly influenced by Haydn's practice of expanding small motifs into a large design, Beethoven also sought to exploit the interrelationships among them. For example, in the luminous C major Adagio movement the exuberant middle section (F major) is based on a short motif derived from the closing material of the first section. Yet what the listener apprehends, especially in the final two movements, is an overall mood of good humor and high spirits. Beethoven described the finale as *aufgeknöpft* (unbuttoned), suggesting a free and informal character.

String Quartet in D Major, Opus 18 No. 3

Allegro
Andante con moto
Allegro
Presto

The D Major Quartet unfolds with ease and elegance, but Beethoven's sketchbooks reveal the intensive labor of its creation. The first of the Opus 18 set to be completed, this quartet shows his new mastery of counterpoint—a high baroque technique of combining diverse but complementary lines. Beethoven described counterpoint as "a hard nut, but one that must be cracked" in order to create the intricate yet clear texture he desired. Despite this quartet's songful obeisance to Mozart, Beethoven's innovative details permeate the work. Each of the lyrical Allegro's two themes begins in harmonies unorthodox for their time, leading critics to charge that Beethoven had violated tonal rules. In the eloquent Andante con moto movement (B flat major), Beethoven inventively references earlier themes—for example, in its recapitulation the second theme functions as a bass accompaniment for the first theme.

As a departure from the classical scherzo, Beethoven's third movement is a gentle intermezzo (D major) with a mysterious contrasting section in D minor. The vigorous Presto finale, which suggests good-natured rustic dance, opens with an incisive three-note motif that sustains its momentum until the whispering conclusion.

String Quartet in C Minor, Opus 18 No. 4

Allegro ma non tanto
Scherzo: Andante scherzoso quasi allegretto
Menuetto: Allegretto
Allegro

A brief anecdote told about Opus 18 No. 4 in C Minor illustrates Beethoven's revolutionary spirit. His pupil Ferdinand Ries writes: "One day as I was walking with him I mentioned an instance of the classically forbidden parallel fifths in the quartet's finale. Beethoven thought I was mistaken, so I wrote out the passage on the ruled paper he always carried. Beethoven remarked, 'Well! Who says that parallel fifths are wrong?' I listed the many theorists. Beethoven replied, 'No matter. I allow use of them!'"

Opus 18 No. 4, the only minor key work in the set, emerges as the most typically "Beethovenian" of the group because of its heightened drama. Early in his career Beethoven often used the key of C minor for works with a tragic cast, such as the Opus 13 *Sonata pathétique*. It is possible that the turbulent C Minor Quartet was written in response to his increasing deafness, which he began to realize as early as 1796.

The passionately intense Allegro opens with a driving theme in the first violin. The second violin states the second subject (E flat major), derived from the latter part of the opening theme. As this sonata form movement develops, its themes achieve an orchestral effect through repeated notes in the inner voices. The ideas are restated with energetic syncopations, and the movement ends with a coda dramatized by a long crescendo.

The moderately paced Scherzo replaces the traditional slow movement. Its three themes, developed through imitation, all include a memorable figure of three repeating notes. The influence of Mozart is heard in the Menuetto, in which alternating sforzandi in the opening phrase echo the classical master's K. 387 Menuetto.

Its middle section is a songful duet between the second violin and viola, accompanied by triplets in the first violin. The opening material returns in a faster tempo.

The C minor finale is a rondo in the style of Haydn. The first theme suggests the popular Turkish style, and the second idea provides a lyrical contrast. After three returns of the material, the work concludes with a prestissimo coda.

String Quartet in A Major, Opus 18 No. 5

Allegro
Menuetto
Andante cantabile
Allegro

Beethoven was inspired to write his Opus 18 No. 5 after hearing Mozart's innovative Quartet in A Major, K. 464 (1785), a technically brilliant yet profound work written to honor Haydn. Seeing the score for the first time in 1800, Beethoven was heard to exclaim: "That's what I call a work! Mozart is telling the world, 'Look what I could do if you were ready for it!' " To absorb Mozart's compositional techniques Beethoven wrote out a copy of K. 464's score. Soon afterwards Beethoven began sketches for his Opus 18 No. 5.

The Allegro opens with a graceful group of themes that evoke Mozart's songful idiom. A contrasting subject follows in the minor mode. After development of these ideas, the opening material is recapitulated and the movement concludes with a brief coda based on a fragmentary A major scale.

Beethoven most often placed his slow movement after the opening Allegro, but in Opus 18 No. 5 he observed Mozart's preference for the Menuetto as the second movement. A delicate waltz, the movement is varied by a three-voice canon and a brusquely accented trio section.

The Andante cantabile explores a simple theme, which

Beethoven described as "pastoral," through five increasingly complex variations. Beethoven moves beyond Classicism's technique of variation achieved through altered embellishments or rhythms; rather, in Opus 18 No. 5 each variation reveals a dramatic new aspect of theme's character. Especially remarkable is the robust fifth variation, which references the emphatic cello drumbeat of Mozart's K. 464. In the substantial coda the theme reappears in its original form against rapid scale figures. Near the end the tempo slows to create a subdued conclusion.

The sonata form Allegro finale is propelled by an incisive four-note motto heard at the outset. At its center a thematic link to Mozart's A Major Quartet finale is heard in long note values.

String Quartet in B flat Major, Opus 18 No. 6

Allegro con brio
Adagio ma non troppo
Scherzo: Allegro
La Malinconia (Adagio)—Allegretto quasi allegro

The B flat Major Quartet, the last of the Opus 18 set, is distinguished by its finale's brief and sorrowful introduction, which Beethoven entitled "Melancholy." Many listeners have interpreted this harmonically adventuresome section, which Beethoven wrote should be played "with the greatest delicacy," as Romanticism's true beginning. Surprisingly, its tragic atmosphere is quickly dispelled by the convivial Allegretto that quickly follows—an abrupt mood shift that is a hallmark of Beethoven's later work.

The Allegro con brio opens with a simple motif treated as a good-natured duet between the violin and cello. As heard in the quartets of Haydn, the development unfolds dramatically with bold harmonic excursions and effective pauses before new ideas. The serene Adagio (E flat major) develops its two contrasting ideas in three-part song form. The violin line grows ever more florid; the cello alternates between lyrical statements and strong rhythmic punctuations. The Scherzo (B flat major) is energized by syncopations and unexpected accents. The smooth trio section offers a brief respite from these rhythmic complexities before the Scherzo returns for a literal repeat.

MIDDLE QUARTETS (1805–1814)

The Rasumovsky Quartets, Opus 59 Nos. 1–3 (1806)

Perhaps the most musically conversant of Beethoven's aristocratic patrons was Count Andrey Rasumovsky, the Russian son of the Empress Catherine's "favorite" and recipient of a lifetime ambassadorship to the Hapsburg Court at Vienna. An accomplished amateur violinist and cellist who maintained a superb string quartet as part of his household staff, Rasumovsky commissioned Beethoven to write three quartets for concerts intended to serve a dual purpose—both to celebrate his palatial new embassy, grandly adorned with statuary by Canova, and also to commemorate the grievous 1805 Austro-Russian military defeat by Napoleon at Austerlitz, which left thousands of his countrymen dead. Rasumovsky stipulated that each of the quartets include Russian themes as a patriotic gesture, and Beethoven searched for appropriate melodies to honor this request. Although engaged with other large-scale projects of his productive "middle period," Beethoven devoted his full attention to the commission, and he soon completed his Opus 59 (1806). These "Rasumovsky" Quartets mark a new era for the string quartet. Formerly a genre written for intimate chambers, the string quartet is here an expanded, quasi-orchestral form intended for a concert hall with a large audience.

Beethoven at this time was obsessed by his desire to master sonata form—an established, yet flexible, eighteenth-century scheme that provided large works with a coherent structure: the exposition of ideas, their full development, their return in mostly original form, and an extensive coda. This clear framework allowed Beethoven to create dramatically nuanced, spacious designs with maximum thematic and harmonic contrast. Each of the Rasumovsky Quartets features at least the opening movement in sonata form. Remarkably, in the first quartet of the set each of its four movements is so constructed.

String Quartet in F Major, Opus 59 No. 1

Allegro
Allegretto vivace e sempre scherzando
Adagio molto e mesto
Thème russe: Allegro

Perhaps because Rasumovsky favored the cello, the monumental Allegro opens with a forthright statement in the cello's middle register. This boldly confident theme is continued by the violin, which soon introduces the second subject. A codetta leads to the vast and imaginative development section, which includes a fugal section at its center. The cello begins the recapitulation, which is subtly linked to the development by overlying passages in the violin. Returning ideas are varied and expanded in both the recapitulation and the concluding coda.

The second movement also begins with a cello statement, but one that struck the Count's resident quartet as a very poor joke—a solo rhythmic figure on the note B flat. Although launched by ostensibly unpromising material, this scherzo movement develops with wit and lyricism.

The profound Adagio is a sonata form movement of unprecedented length. In his sketches Beethoven wrote the words "A weeping willow or acacia tree upon my brother's grave." Perhaps an allusion to a brother who had died in infancy, the inscription suggests that the movement should be heard as a sustained lament. The cello eloquently sings its two themes in the upper register. The violin shares the material, which is developed through brilliant scoring and varied accompaniments. Runs in the violin connect the movement to the Allegro finale, which begins with a vivacious Russian theme. Beethoven evidently found the melody in a collection of Russian folk songs; originally a slow tune in D minor, the song here is a rapid statement in F major. A second theme is introduced and the material is treated canonically. A sudden adagio stops the momentum, but the vivacity soon returns to conclude the movement.

String Quartet in E Minor, Opus 59 No. 2

Allegro
Molto adagio
Allegretto (Thème russe)
Finale: Presto

Beethoven wrote much of Opus 59 No. 2 during his 1806 summer visit to the Graz castle of his patron, Prince Lichnowsky. There he worked with such fierce absorption that the castle staff described him as "not in his right mind." The visit ended abruptly after Lichnowsky asked Beethoven to perform for several French officers enjoying leisure after their victory over the Russians and Austrians at Austerlitz. Beethoven refused to perform, and he and the Prince quarreled. With his patronage in jeopardy, the enraged Beethoven set off for Vienna despite a heavy rainstorm, which slightly damaged his new manuscripts.

Inward and mysterious, the compact sonata form Allegro of Opus 59 No. 2 begins with two terse chords followed by wisps of a theme. Although subsequent reiterations are gradually woven into an extended melodic line, shifting rhythms and numerous short pauses create an aura of uncertainty that is only resolved at the assertive coda.

The eloquent Adagio molto, also in sonata form, develops a theme possibly derived from the musical spelling of Bach's name, which in German is B flat, A, C, B natural. According to Beethoven's friend Czerny, this movement occurred to its composer "when contemplating the starry sky and thinking of music of the spheres." As homage to Rasumovsky, the Allegretto showcases the Russian patriotic hymn *Slava* ("Glory") in its trio section. The brilliant finale, in sonata rondo form, gains tension with unexpected harmonic relationships. Most probably a programmatic movement, one might hear the Czar's stallions galloping to the front in its spectacular coda.

String Quartet in C Major, Opus 59 No. 3

Introduzione: Andante con moto—Allegro vivace
Andante con moto quasi Allegretto
Menuetto: Grazioso
Allegro molto

Opus 59 No. 3, like each of Beethoven's middle period quartets, opens with a sonata form movement that grounds his adventurous thematic explorations and exploits contrasts of theme and harmony to achieve varying nuances of mood. After a slow and harmonically enigmatic introduction, a solid C major key center is established at the Allegro vivace, which develops two exuberant themes. Near the conclusion the dynamics increase from very soft to very loud as the tempo accelerates, creating an impressive coda.

Unlike the first two Rasumovsky Quartets, Opus 59 No. 3 does not feature identifiable Russian themes. However, the elegiac slow movement (A minor) conjures the essence of a Ukrainian folk melody with its characteristic melodic interval structure.

Underpinned by steady pizzicati in the cello, the movement develops with subtle harmonic modulations. The graceful Menuetto (C major) is varied by a rhythmically incisive trio section (F major). An echo of the quartet's introduction, a harmonically ambiguous bridge connects this movement to the finale. Clarity returns at the substantial Allegro molto, one of the most exciting movements in the quartet literature. A dynamic fugue that develops in sonata form, the movement surges forward with ever-increasing force and energy until its triumphant conclusion.

String Quartet in E flat Major, Opus 74 ("Harp")

Poco Adagio—Allegro
Adagio ma non troppo
Presto
Allegretto con variazioni

The Opus 74 String Quartet was written in 1809, a year of significant events for Beethoven. Three noblemen—Prince Lobkowitz, Count Kinsky, and the Archduke Rudolph—had banded together to provide the composer with a steady annual income of four thousand florins, and Beethoven was elated. His immediate response was to plan marriage, but he proved to be unskilled at courtship. Compounding his frustrations, Vienna soon suffered its second invasion by the French (the first had ruined the premiere of his opera *Fidelio*). According to Beethoven's biographer Schindler, the furious bouts of shelling "destroyed the inner peace necessary for the execution of large compositions." Possibly because of these distractions, Beethoven does not forge new techniques in his splendid Opus 74 but rather refines his earlier innovations.

After a brief, harmonically enigmatic introduction, a clear E flat tonality is established at the sonata form Allegro. After a statement of the lyrical first theme by the violin, the other instruments introduce an arpeggiated pizzicato figure. Near the end of the development section, this arpeggio motive is extended in range and executed in increasingly faster rhythms to suggest the plucking of a harp—leading to the quartet's nickname "Harp." This theme returns at the coda, a section remarkable for its diabolically difficult violin cadenza.

The sublime Adagio develops a serene theme that returns three times with increasingly complex variations. Harmonically rich episodes intervene between these statements. The movement concludes with a warmly ethereal coda.

The forceful Presto recalls the driving scherzo movement of the Fifth Symphony. A C minor movement with recurring trio sections in C major, the movement presses forward at maximum dynamic levels until its final statement, at which point Beethoven demands the softest possible level of sound. A brief pause leads into the finale, six variations of a gracefully flowing melody.

String Quartet in F Minor, Opus 95 ("Serioso")

Allegro con brio
Allegretto ma non troppo
Allegro assai vivace ma serioso
Larghetto espressivo—Allegretto agitato

Beethoven wrote his Opus 95 string quartet for his friend and confidant Nicholay Zmeskall, an amateur cellist and composer who frequently hosted informal chamber music sessions in his home. Although the work was initially completed in 1810, Beethoven revised it extensively in 1814 and premiered it that year. Before its publication Beethoven wrote in a letter: "The Quartet is written for a small circle of connoisseurs, and it is not to be performed in public." Possibly he issued this directive because he perceived that the quartet was stylistically far ahead of its time and therefore likely to be misunderstood. Although Opus 95 is Beethoven's final middle period quartet chronologically, it reveals characteristics of his final set of quartets, begun ten years later. Most notably there is often similarly terse expression, the result of strongly stated ideas separated by minimal transitions.

Beethoven inscribed the words *Quartetto serioso* on his manuscript and included the word "serious" in the third movement's tempo marking. There is conjecture that this subtitle, as well as the pervasive mood of tragic intensity in Opus 95, stems from Beethoven's unfortunate love affair with the much younger Therese Malfatti during this same year. The quartet shows expressive affinities to the Goethe-inspired *Egmont Overture*, also in F minor, which it immediately followed.

Like his other four middle period quartets, Opus 95 opens with a movement in sonata form. However, the brusquely passionate Allegro con brio is the most condensed and elliptical movement that Beethoven ever wrote in that form. Pared to essentials, the movement eliminates the customary repeat of the exposition. Its two contrasting themes undergo only a brief development and a truncated recapitulation.

The second movement (D major) develops two contrasting ideas, a cantabile theme and a fugato that suggest the opening movement of the much later quartet Opus 131. The third movement, a scherzo with a contrasting trio section at its center, follows without pause. Abrupt and jagged rhythms anticipate patterns heard in the final quartets. The finale's poignant Larghetto introduction, thematically related to the third movement, leads to the Allegretto agitato, which develops two restless subjects in sonata rondo form. After a dramatic ritardando, the mode changes to major and the tempo accelerates to suggest a victorious resolution.

LATE QUARTETS (1824–1826)

During the eight years before Beethoven began his monumental final set of string quartets, he endured a period of spiritual isolation. Because of complete deafness, desertion by earlier patrons, and difficulties with both family and publishers, he often lacked the will to compose. Fortunately, he was galvanized by a commission from Prince Nicholay Galitzin, a Russian nobleman and amateur cellist, for "two or three string quartets, for which labor I will be glad to pay you what you think proper." From May 1824 until November 1826, only four months before his death, Beethoven devoted all his energies to the creation of works for Galitzin (Opp. 127, 130, 132, and 133), as well as two other quartets written without commission (Opp. 131 and 135). Each of these transcendent works explores a musical universe expanded by an unprecedented fluidity of structure that allows each work to develop according to the demands of Beethoven's vision.

String Quartet in E flat Major, Opus 127

Maestoso—Allegro
Adagio, ma non troppo e molto cantabile
Scherzando vivace
Allegro—Allegro comodo

Galitzin was mystified by Opus 127, the first of the commissioned quartets, because of its enormous stylistic differences from the earlier quartets he had admired. Early critics were also puzzled by Opus 127, which suffered from an inadequately rehearsed premiere in March, 1825. There were objections to the level of dissonance, which the deaf composer accepted but which remained uncomfortable to listeners for decades after his death. There was consternation that the work overall appeared to be a web woven from thematic particles rather than a developed set of themes with strong profiles, although these do exist. Unexpected changes of tempo within movements left the audience lost. The prevalent opinion was voiced by one present: "Although we do not understand it, each of us was conscious that we had been in the presence of something higher than ourselves, beyond our capacity to comprehend."

Opus 127, like the other late opus quartets, stands in two differing tonal worlds—the Classic and the Romantic. Initially the work promises to unfold with the coherent regularity characteristic of an earlier classical composition. Yet the work develops with rhythmic subtleties and harmonic ambiguities that obscure the clarity of its underlying structure. The opening Maestoso, while ostensibly similar to many of Beethoven's other introductions, establishes a uniquely questioning mood. These opening measures recur in the following Allegro section (in effect dividing it into three parts), where they function to stabilize the free harmonic scheme of the movement as it develops.

The second movement is a set of five variations based on two deceptively simple themes. These subtly elaborated variations move through daring and remote key modulations to achieve moments of true sublimity.

The incisive rhythms of the Scherzando abruptly bring the listener from this high plane. Unexpected changes of rhythms, dynamics, and mood contribute to a sense of unrest. The finale, a more classical exploration of two folklike themes, restores an atmosphere of clarity. The coda, initiated by a faster tempo, propels the work toward an exhilarating conclusion.

String Quartet in B flat Major, Opus 130

Adagio ma non troppo—Allegro
Presto
Andante con moto ma non troppo
Alla danza tedesca: Allegro assai
Cavatina: Adagio molto espressivo
Finale: Allegro

Beethoven was especially fond of his Opus 130, which he referred to as the Liebquartett (Dear Quartet) in his conversation books. Perhaps because of his deafness he chose not to attend the work's premiere in March, 1826 but rather to wait in a nearby tavern for word of the audience's response. His nephew Karl soon brought positive news that two of the six movements met with such favor that they had to be repeated. Karl also gave less favorable news—the fugal finale confused listeners ("as incomprehensible as Chinese," said one present). Beethoven exploded with anger. Soon after the premiere his publisher and several friends persuaded Beethoven to compose a new, more traditional finale for Opus 130 and to allow the original movement, the *Grosse Fuge* ("Great Fugue"), to stand as a separate composition (now Opus 133).

Although Opus 130 was described by Beethoven's biographer Schindler as "the monster among all quartets," its framework follows the basic four-movement classical pattern. However, Beethoven expands this scheme by adding both a scherzo and a slow movement before the finale. Within these movements thematic material develops with extreme flexibility. Opus 130 begins with a serene Adagio that appears to be a traditional introduction, but it reappears surprisingly between faster statements in the spirited Allegro. The resulting shifts of mood led Aldous Huxley to describe the movement as "majesty alternating with a joke."

The fleet Presto (D flat major) functions as a bridge between the complex opening movement and the rhythmically intricate third movement. Based on short and repeated melodic units, the Presto unfolds with contrasting simplicity.

The following Andante (D flat major, marked "moderately slow with motion, but not too much") combines levity with wistful melancholy. The viola states the principal theme, marked "a little playfully," in its lower register. The violins develop melodies and countermelodies continuously underpinned by rhythmic figuration in the cello.

The fluent Alla danza tedesca (Dance in the German Style, G major) functions as a second scherzo. It resembles a gentle Ländler, a rustic triple-time German dance.

Cavatina ("little aria") is an outpouring of heartfelt song. This brief movement begins with calm serenity but steadily gains intensity until its poignant harmonic shift from C flat major to A flat minor—at which place Beethoven penned the word "anguished" in the manuscript. His friend Karl Holz wrote that the Cavatina was composed "amid sorrow and tears; never did his music breathe so deep an inspiration, and even the memory of this movement brought tears to his eyes." (A Budapest Quartet recording of the Cavatina was included in the Golden Record for Voyager's interstellar journey, commenced in 1977.)

The Allegro finale (B flat major), the movement substituted for the *Grosse Fuge*, stands as Beethoven's final composition. Despite ongoing illness and discomfort, Beethoven crafted an ostensibly good-humored sonata form movement that alludes to the quartet's earlier themes and harmonic relationships.

Grosse Fuge, Opus 133

The remarkable *Grosse Fuge*, published posthumously as Opus 133 in 1827, is often performed as the original finale of Opus 130. This intense and driving "Great Fugue" begins with an overture (Allegro, G major) that introduces the concise, somewhat jagged, motto theme. After a variation of this theme in a brief passage marked "less motion, moderate tempo," the powerful fugue begins to develop (Allegro, B flat major). The motto passes in turn from the first violin to the second violin, then to the viola and cello. A variation of the motto becomes a countersubject to the main theme. The fugue builds over a tremendous crescendo and comes to a dramatic pause. A quieter variant of the motto is developed in a pianissimo section again marked "less motion, moderate tempo" (G flat major). The fugue returns at a fortissimo section marked "very fast and with spirit" (B flat major). After a robust development that emphasizes the fervent and jagged character of the theme, the marking "less motion, moderate tempo" returns (F minor). The tempo gradually accelerates, and the marking "very fast and with spirit" returns. On the final pages the themes are transformed into a dance of victory.

Throughout the fugue one hears unique thematic links to the quartet's earlier movements—compelling evidence that the *Grosse Fuge* belongs to Opus 130 as its appropriate finale.

String Quartet in C sharp Minor, Opus 131

Adagio, ma non troppo e molto espressivo
Allegro molto vivace
Allegro moderato
Andante, ma non troppo e molto cantabile
Presto
Adagio quasi un poco andante
Allegro

A profound and mystical work that Beethoven considered to be one of his greatest compositions, Opus 131 was begun after he received a commission from Schott and Sons Publishers in 1826. The completed score was sent with a note: "Fourth quartet of the newest ones. Purloined and assembled from various sources, hither and yon." Beethoven's flippancy so alarmed the publishers that he soon sent a second note: "You wrote that this was to be an original quartet, and this annoyed me. I jocularly wrote otherwise, but in fact it is brand-new." Beethoven was in fact meticulous about his publishing arrangements. Only six months after this exchange, in the throes of his final illness he directed that a letter be drafted to Schott clarifying his proprietary rights to Opus 131.

A glance at the work's unusual structure—seven connected movements offering dramatic emotional contrast—shows radical differences from what he had written before. Beethoven was most probably influenced by the growing force of literary Romanticism and its experimentation with the "fragment," a text intentionally left incomplete so that the reader must actively reflect upon it. In the C sharp Minor Quartet Beethoven breaks down the concept of "movement" as an independent statement, for several of the sections are too fleeting to stand alone. Instead he shapes the work through a fluid succession of forms, often brief, to create one large, coherent statement. In actual time Opus 131 is no longer than his middle period quartets, but it is far more varied in terms of key scheme, moods, and textures.

Planning the sequence of movements doubtless represented a large part of Beethoven's creative process. The fugal opening movement, which shares thematic material and key orientation with the finale, functions as a contemplative introduction. The rapid second movement provides a cheerful contrast. Movement III, a rhythmically free recitative, links the Allegro vivace to the Andante, a theme and variations movement remarkable for its exploration of instrumental textures. The playful Presto corresponds to a classical scherzo movement. Movement VI, a 28-bar adagio possibly based on an old French song, offers a deeply introspective transition between the two fast movements. The powerful finale was eloquently described by Richard Wagner: "This is the fury of the world's dance ... and above the tumult the indomitable fiddler whirls us on to the abyss. To him it is nothing but a mocking fantasy; at the end darkness beckons him away, and his task is done."

String Quartet in A Minor, Opus 132

Assai sostenuto—Allegro
Allegro ma non tanto
Heiliger Danksgesang eines Genesenden an die Gottheit,
    in der lydischen Tonart: Molto adagio Neue Kraft
    fühlend: Andante
Alla Marcia, assai vivace
Allegro appassionato

Opus 132 is the second of the six monumental string quartets Beethoven began in 1824 and completed only four months before his death. During this late phase of his career, Beethoven had negotiated with the London Philharmonic Society, which hoped to lure him to England as composer-in-residence. Frustrated by the low fees offered, Beethoven reluctantly terminated these discussions and focused on the generous commission from Prince Nicholay Galitzin. However, as he became deeply involved with the quartets' creation, Beethoven gradually grew oblivious to his benefactor. He ignored Galitzin's correspondence and indeed appeared to forget his existence. The Prince was infuriated to learn that the premiere of Opus 132 (1825) was held without his having been notified.

During the composition of Opus 132, Beethoven had become seriously ill, most probably with liver disease, and was confined to bed for an entire month. His sketchbooks show that he had intended to construct Opus 132 in a traditional four-movement format. However, upon recovery he decided to add a central movement, the "Convalescent's Holy Song of Thanksgiving to the Deity," as an expression of gratitude for his restored health. The inclusion of this fifth movement, a statement of his humble yet fervent appreciation for life, contributes a deeply spiritual dimension to the entire quartet.

The quartet's slow introduction begins with a four-note motif in the cello—an ascending half step followed by an upward leap. (One of the many constructive links among these organically unified quartets, this motif resembles themes heard in the Opus 130 and Opus 131 quartets, which were sketched at the same time but actually completed after Opus 132.) This portentous motif returns between the three main thematic ideas of the Allegro, a sonata form movement remarkable in its flexibility. The second movement is a wistful scherzo that grows from two melodic cells. After a pastoral musette suggesting a bagpipe drone, the opening material returns.

Beethoven wrote his third movement in the ancient Lydian mode, which corresponds to the modern F major scale without the B flat. Constructed as a five-part aria, the movement alternates between the hymn and faster sections that programmatically depict the invalid's strength returning ("Neue Kraft fühlend"). A brief march movement follows. After a rhythmically free violin recitative, the rondo finale, "fast and impassioned," reaches an exuberant conclusion as the mode changes from A minor to A major.

String Quartet in F Major, Opus 135

Allegretto
Vivace
Lento assai, cantante e tranquillo
Grave, ma non troppo tratto—Allegro (Der schwer gefasste
    Entschluss: Muss es sein? Es muss sein! Es muss sein!)

Beethoven composed his Opus 135 (1826), his sixteenth and final string quartet, during his summer visit to the Austrian countryside. This buoyant F major quartet offers a classical contrast to the romantic sensibility of its powerful predecessor in C sharp minor (Opus 131), composed that same year. The relatively lessened intensity of Opus 135 reflects a pattern that Beethoven had established over the course of his career—to follow the creation of a forceful work with one that projects an aura of calm and repose.

The convivial opening movement (Allegretto) develops its five concise motifs in the inventive manner of Haydn, who inspired Beethoven early in his career. These ideas are exchanged among the instruments as if they were engaged in informal conversation. The Vivace, a scherzo movement, is notable for its brusque phrase interruptions and also its relentless ostinato—in the movement's central section, the first violin executes a virtuoso line over a figure that is repeated forty-seven times by the other instruments, a tour de force that must have been heard as deranged by his early listeners. The Lento assai (D flat major) consists of four variations on a theme described by Beethoven as "a sweet, restful, peaceful song."

Beethoven prefaced his finale with the words "The decision made with difficulty." To continue the enigma, under the emphatic notes of the primary motif (marked "Grave") he wrote: "Must it be? It must be!" The argument persists as to whether these words signal an aging composer's resignation or only a pretense to seriousness. Although Beethoven actually did write his publisher that the composition of the last movement represented "a difficult decision," the phrase most probably has humorous origins. The story goes that Beethoven had refused to give his friend Ignaz Dembscher a copy of an earlier quartet because he had not attended its premiere. A mutual friend suggested that Dembscher soothe the composer's wounded feelings by paying his performers 50 florins, thereby underwriting the new concert. Dembscher asked, "Muss es sein?" The friend replied, "Es muss sein!" When Beethoven heard of this exchange, he burst into laughter and immediately began to write a canon on the dialogue. He later expanded this motivic material to create the final movement of Opus 135.

FIVE

The Lyrical Romantic: Schubert's Chamber Works

FRANZ SCHUBERT
B. JAN. 31, 1797 IN VIENNA,
D. NOV. 19, 1828 IN VIENNA

The days of Schubert's outwardly uneventful and too brief life were consumed by his incessant composition. "As soon as I have completed a piece I take up manuscript paper and begin another," he said. However, his evenings were enlivened by wonderful chamber music sessions with his musician friends. These *Schubertiaden*, at times held almost nightly, offered their composer his primary opportunity to hear and evaluate his work. Schubert himself played both violin and viola in the groups, but the piano was his preferred instrument: "People assure me that the keys become singing voices under my fingers," he stated with satisfaction. Certainly, Schubert received highest praise for his piano works: "Particularly as a composer for the piano he has stood out," wrote Robert Schumann. "Everything sounds so appropriately and inherently from the very heart of the piano." However, Schubert focused his major effort on the string quartet form, which he perceived as critical to his ongoing development as a symphonic composer: "I intend to pave my way toward the grand symphony through the string quartet," he wrote. Because of his untimely death Schubert's projected "grand symphonies" were never written, but listeners value the enduring legacy of his existing symphonies and chamber works.

STRING QUARTETS

String Quartet in A Minor, D. 804 ("Rosamunde")

Allegro ma non troppo
Andante
Menuetto: Allegretto
Allegro moderato

Only one of Schubert's string quartets was published during his lifetime—his great String Quartet in A Minor, D. 804. This quartet, the first that Schubert had conceived for performance by a professional ensemble, was begun in 1824 shortly after he had undergone treatment for a venereal infection. Exhausted and discouraged, he wrote to a friend describing his emotional state: "Think of a man whose health will never be right again, and whose despair over this makes it worse; think of a man whose hopes have come to naught, to whom the happiness of love offers nothing but the most acute pain." His despondency is most probably reflected in his gently melancholy A Minor Quartet.

The quartet's first three movements develop themes that had appeared in Schubert's earlier works. The Allegro non troppo opens with an undulating second violin figure that introduces the main theme, played by the first violin. This subsidiary figure is heard in Schubert's early song *Gretchen at the Spinning Wheel* and underpins the words "My peace is gone, my heart is heavy, I'll find it never, never again." After a brief transition, a wistful second subject is heard in the second violin. An extensive development section explores the first idea, now heightened emotionally by dramatic harmonic modulations.

Schubert was especially fond of the lyrical Andante, originally conceived as incidental music for Helmina von Chézy's four-act play *Rosamunde, Princess of Cyprus*—a theatrical disaster terminated after two performances. Perhaps he reworked this material to insure its survival in another genre.

The Menuetto opens with a brooding motive in the cello's lowest register; the other strings echo and extend the idea. Schubert had used this theme in his 1820 song *Die Götter Griechenlands* ("The Greek Gods"). Possibly he now embraced the lyrics to the song, a plea for the return of youth: "Where art thou, beautiful world? Come again, glorious age of Nature." The somber tone of the Menuetto continues in its trio section, notable for its poignant cello passage.

The buoyant finale sets an exuberant mood. Its two themes, derived from Hungarian folk music, are brilliantly developed by all four instruments.

String Quartet in D Minor, D. 810 ("Death and the Maiden")

Allegro
Andante con moto
Scherzo: Allegro molto
Presto

Schubert drafted his D. 810 Quartet in March 1824 but because of his dispirited frame of mind he set it aside for two years. Finally galvanized by a desperate need for income, he decided in February 1826 to polish the quartet for its premiere and publication. Although Schubert enjoyed performing as quartet violist, he instead devoted his energies to revisions of D. 810 during the two rehearsals of the work. Four weeks later he offered the quartet to the Schott publishing firm, but it was rejected. The quartet was finally published in 1831, three years after Schubert's death.

As was typical of Romantic composers, Schubert frequently based an instrumental composition on his own song motives. The second movement of D. 810 develops Schubert's 1817 song *Der Tod und das Mädchen* ("Death and the Maiden"), in which a gentle figure of Death arrives to claim the life of a young girl. Perhaps correctly, many commentators have observed that the central position of this song suggests that the entire D. 810 conveys Schubert's own views on death. Yet there is evidence that Schubert simply chose the song at the urging of friends who admired the melody.

The Allegro explores two contrasting motives, the first ominous and rhythmically forceful, the second warmly lyrical. The substantial coda builds to a forceful climax, but the movement ends quietly. The somber second movement explores the eponymous song theme through five variations. Its serene, major-key conclusion conveys an atmosphere of peaceful ascension. The syncopated and rhythmically vibrant Scherzo is varied by its graceful and songlike trio section. The movement concludes with a literal repeat of the opening material. The Presto finale resembles a tarantella, a frenzied Italian dance that wards off death with ever faster movement.

String Quartet in G Major, D. 887

Allegro molto moderato
Andante un poco moto
Scherzo: Allegro vivace
Allegro assai

Schubert's D. 887 Quartet in G Major is the last of his fifteen string quartets and perhaps the most remarkable. Within a ten-day period in June 1826 Schubert created a towering work of astounding modernity from the briefest of thematic ideas. Recognizing its uniqueness, he chose to program the quartet's first movement on the breakthrough invitational concert held six months before his death. Although the critics present praised its "spirit and originality," publishers rejected the work because of its length and difficulty. The quartet was eventually published posthumously fifteen years after its completion.

A restless, questioning atmosphere is established at the outset. The quartet begins with a harmonically ambiguous motif—a sustained opening chord in G major abruptly resolves on G minor, followed by a staccato response. The second theme, a poignant utterance played in short, syncopated phrases by the violin, is repeated by the cello. Freely cast in sonata form, the movement unfolds within a framework of harmonies that continuously alternate between the major and minor modes. Agitated tremolos and virtuoso passagework contribute to the orchestral quality of this extensive movement.

The last three movements of D. 887 reveal relationships to Schubert's D. 810 String Quartet in D minor ("Death and the Maiden"), premiered in January of the same year. While the earlier Andante is clearly based on the titular song in which Death comes to claim a young girl, the dramatic Andante (E minor) of D. 887 might also suggest a programmatic interpretation. After the cello's wistfully melancholy opening solo, the first section develops as an ordered world. But suddenly, in the second thematic area (G minor), a violent Schubert emerges. Abruptly loud phrases with jagged rhythms and vehemently roiling melodic cells, made even more emphatic by their separating rests, conjure a devastating operatic scene.

The Scherzo (B minor) returns to Schubert's more familiar world. A buoyant melodic idea is followed by a central trio section (G major) that resembles a Ländler, a genial Austrian peasant dance. This slower and lilting area offers one of Schubert's characteristic glorious modulations (here to B major) before the repeat of the Scherzo.

The turbulent finale unfolds with relentless energy. Formally this substantial movement is a rondo with two themes and two contrasting interludes. The harmonic ambiguity heard in the opening movement now returns as the key center continuously vacillates between major and minor. As in the earlier "Death and the Maiden" Quartet, its first subject resembles a tarantella, a rapid Italian dance originally executed to purge venom from a spider's victim. The strongly accented second subject perpetuates the momentum of a feverish dance.

WORKS WITH VARIED SCORING

Piano Trio in B flat Major, D. 898

Allegro moderato
Andante un poco mosso
Scherzo: Allegro
Rondo: Allegro vivace

Composers of Schubert's generation tended to avoid creating large-scale piano trio works, either because of intimidation by the genius of Beethoven's 1811 "Archduke" Trio or because of cool responses from publishers catering to a popular market. However, Franz Schubert remained optimistic that publishers would accept his works because of their grand scope and unsurpassed lyricism. Sadly, publishers judged his D. 898 Piano Trio as too difficult for their audience, and the work was published posthumously in 1836.

Written in the productive year preceding Schubert's early death, D. 898 is a radiant masterwork. Schubert boldly resumed trio composition at the point where Beethoven left off, following the forms established by Beethoven but exploring their structures with unexpected turns. Whereas in the earlier phase of piano trio writing the piano and violin were equal voices supported by the cello, Schubert in D. 898 follows Beethoven's practice of forging the strings into a unit that balances the strength of the piano.

The Allegro moderato opens with a lyrical theme played in octaves by the strings and animated by rhythmic figuration in the piano. Its second theme, a broad cantabile melody, is introduced in the upper range of the cello. The opening melody, played forte in the minor key, introduces the development section. Perhaps as a mischievous touch, three false recapitulations occur before the opening theme returns in the correct key. A short coda concludes the movement.

Earlier in 1827 Schubert had composed his D. 897 Notturno, a simple and charming movement intended to be the Andante for D. 898. After D. 898 began to emerge as a more ambitious project, Schubert set the Notturno aside and created a larger new second movement. Here the cello, accompanied by the piano, sings the opening theme as an operatic aria. The other instruments articulate phrases against expressive counterstatements. In the contrasting central area the piano introduces a haunting, habanera-like theme against compelling syncopations in the strings.

The opening section of the Scherzo is energized by playful rhythms; its waltzlike trio section provides a melodic interlude. The primary theme of the joyful concluding Rondo resembles Schubert's earlier song *Skolie* ("Drinking Song"), D. 306, which includes the lyrics, "Let us in the bright May morning take delight in the brief life of the flower, before its fragrance disappears."

Piano Trio in E flat Major, D. 929

Allegro
Andante con moto
Scherzo: Allegro moderato
Allegro moderato

Although Schubert's two late piano trios are now considered to be cornerstones of the trio repertoire, only his D. 929 Trio in E flat (composed in November 1827) was published. When Schubert submitted the work to the publisher Probst in 1828, he attached the following note: "This work will not be dedicated to any special person, but rather to all who find pleasure in it. That is the most profitable form of dedication." Probst offered a curt reply: "I still hope that you will shortly accede to my request to send me trifles for the voice or four hands, a trio being as a rule but an honorary article and rarely capable of bringing in anything." For his monumental E flat Trio Schubert received the small sum of sixty gulden, much of which he paid to his copyist.

Schubert's model for the two piano trios was Beethoven's "Archduke" Trio of 1811, the genius of which, as previously noted, discouraged many contemporary composers from tackling the form. Schubert continues Beethoven's practice of forging the strings into a cohesive unit that balances the strength of the piano. Also like Beethoven he grounds the work with a profound slow movement; in D. 929 this important Andante theme is incorporated into the finale as a unifying device.

The Allegro begins boldly as the instruments play the first of the three main themes in unison. This expansive movement is notable for its large-scale development section, in which a variation of the first theme moves through various tonalities as the piano provides a rippling accompaniment. The remarkable C minor Andante was perhaps inspired by a popular Swedish song that Schubert heard sung by a visiting tenor the previous year. The cello intones an elegiac melody over a solemn, marchlike rhythm in the piano; the violin offers a second theme.

The Scherzo features a canon between the strings and the piano in which the themes are echoed at the octave a measure later. The buoyant finale develops three melodic ideas: a folklike theme that resembles an Austrian Ländler; a Hungarian theme first heard in the piano; and the elegiac melody from the second movement. The movement concludes with a vigorous coda.

Quintet in A Major for Piano, Violin, Viola, Cello, and Double Bass, D. 667 ("Trout")

Allegro vivace
Andante
Scherzo: Presto
Andantino—Allegretto
Allegro giusto

After a walking trip through Upper Austria in the summer of 1819, Schubert wrote his "Trout" Quintet in the picturesque town of Steyr. It has been suggested that the beautiful countryside was a secret collaborator in the Quintet, a work admired for its haunting melodies and radiant spirit. The Quintet was commissioned by the town's musical patron, Sylvester Paumgartner, a prosperous mine manager and accomplished amateur cellist. Paumgartner, who frequently hosted musical evenings in his home, requested its specific instrumentation because friends had recently enjoyed playing Johann Nepomuk Hummel's quintet for the same unusual scoring. Since Paumgartner admired Schubert's 1817 strophic song *Die Forelle* ("The Trout"), he also requested that the composer include a variation movement based on its theme. Schubert was delighted by the prospect of an appreciative audience for his work, and within weeks he had both completed the score and had written out the lengthy parts for the individual players.

The "Trout" Quintet is essentially a lyrical serenade for chamber ensemble. Throughout the work, graceful interplay among the five instruments creates an atmosphere of sociable conversation. The animated Allegro vivace opens with a dramatic arpeggio in the piano, followed by a more serene string melody. Expansion of these ideas leads to a songful duet between the violin and cello. After a harmonically rich development section and a restatement of themes, the movement ends without a coda.

The Andante consists of three contrasting sections, the second of which explores a Magyar-type theme derived from an idea heard in the first movement. The Scherzo opens with an energetic four note motto, a theme that is developed in passages alternately tempestuous and calm.

The fourth movement offers six variations on the opening portion of Schubert's song *Die Forelle*. Stated by the strings alone, the melody is varied and ornamented first in the upper octave of the piano, then by the viola and cello, followed by the double bass. The theme is substantially altered in the fourth and fifth variations, which move into hauntingly remote harmonic areas. In the final variation the song appears in its original form with the piano articulating a rippling accompaniment. The finale, "in the Hungarian style," develops two lively themes, the second of which recalls the Quintet's opening movement.

String Quintet in C Major, D.956 ("Cello Quintet")

Allegro ma non troppo
Adagio
Scherzo: Presto—Trio: Andante sostenuto
Allegretto

Schubert's String Quintet in C Major is regarded as one of the greatest of all chamber compositions because of its ethereally beautiful melodies and wide range of emotion. Schubert wrote his D. 956 Quintet during the late summer of 1828, his productive final year of life. He submitted the work to publishers but died before knowing that it had been rejected. Since its manuscript languished for years in private hands, the D. 956 premiere was held twenty-two years after Schubert's death. Publication occurred another three years later.

Warmly romantic lyricism and poetic intimacy characterize the Quintet. Because of the addition of the second cello to the standard string quartet format, the work glows with rich sonorities.

This unusual instrumental combination allows one cello to share fully the thematic material, often in octaves with the first violin, to create consistently strong melodic lines. At moments a nearly orchestral effect is achieved.

The Quintet opens with daring simplicity—a C major chord that grows from very soft to very loud. After the first violin offers a brief melodic extension, the material is restated in D minor. This unusual departure from the key area both transforms the motive's character and signals that bold harmonic excursions lie ahead. The second subject, a songful duet for the two cellos, creates the emotional center of the exposition. After an expansive development and a free recapitulation of themes, the movement concludes with a brief coda.

The sublime Adagio (E major) begins with measured slowness that conjures ethereal suspension. Pizzicati in the second cello provide rhythmic underpinning. A sudden trill signals the turbulent middle section (F minor). The first violin and the first cello, now in its highest register, sing the passionate theme as the other instruments articulate agitated accompaniments. The opening material (E major) returns, now ornamented with elaborate ascending lines in the second cello.

An exuberant rustic dance launches the Scherzo (C major). Unexpected accents provide subtle rhythmic play. Suggestions of hunting horns lend orchestral character. Suddenly, at the Andante sostenuto (D flat major), the atmosphere becomes profoundly introspective. A harmonically free lament, the Trio grows increasingly somber as the instruments descend in their registers. A hushed transition leads to a return of the extroverted opening material.

The lighthearted sonata rondo finale develops two themes, one evoking Hungarian folk music and a second suggesting Viennese dance. Near its conclusion the two cellos sing a poignant duet, accompanied primarily by the viola line, as a reference to the second subject of the first movement. The tempo then accelerates and the Quintet concludes with a luminous coda.

Octet in F Major for Two Violins, Viola, Cello, Double Bass,
Clarinet, Bassoon, and Horn, D. 803

Adagio—Allegro
Adagio
Allegro vivace
Andante
Menuetto: Allegretto
Andante molto—Allegro

Schubert endured periods of melancholy during his mature years due to poor health and lack of recognition or income from his compositions. "Every night when I go to bed I hope I might not wake up," he once wrote. However, he became euphoric when he received a commission from the eminent Count Ferdinand Troyer, an official in the court of Archduke Rudolph. Troyer, an accomplished amateur clarinetist, wished to expand the limited chamber repertoire for his instrument. He had performed Beethoven's popular Opus 20 Septet (1800), and he desired an entertaining companion to this radiant work. Troyer requested that Schubert duplicate the Septet's style and format, and he agreed to the addition of a second violin for enhanced sonority. Schubert quickly immersed himself in this project, which was to be his largest-scale chamber work. His friends observed: "Schubert works with the greatest zeal on his Octet. If you go to see him, he says 'How are you? Good!' And you depart." Schubert was pleased with his Octet (completed in March 1824) and he submitted it to several publishers. Unfortunately, they rejected the work, and the Octet was published posthumously in 1853.

The Octet delighted its audience at Troyer's home premiere, and its similarity to Beethoven's Septet was much appreciated. Both works unfold in a six-movement scheme that recalls the tuneful eighteenth-century divertimento style especially enjoyed by the Viennese. Schubert closely followed the Septet's key relationships, and he digressed only slightly from the Septet's movement sequence by adjusting the positions of the Menuetto and Scherzo. Yet despite his adherence to Beethoven's classical model, Schubert's uniquely romantic spirit pervades the Octet.

Structurally, the Octet resembles an eighteenth-century serenade, a succession of melodious movements framed by two marches that suggest the assembling and departures of players. The Octet opens with a substantial sonata form movement pervaded with emphatic dotted rhythms that perhaps allude to the serenade's origins as "strolling" music. Initially heard in the slow introduction, the dotted figuration expands to become the primary theme of the Allegro; the clarinet introduces the calmer second theme of this spirited movement. The introductory material returns at the recapitulation, and the movement concludes with a rapid coda.

Curiously, the second movement is marked Adagio (slow) in Schubert's 1824 manuscript but Andante un poco mosso (moderately slow with some motion) in the posthumous first publication. This lyrical movement (B flat major), written in three-part song form, opens with a pensive clarinet statement; a trio section (C major) offers thematic contrast. A rustic dance, the Allegro vivace (movement III) is propelled by strongly dotted rhythms; a songful trio section provides contrast. The following Andante (movement IV) consists of seven variations on a theme from Schubert's opera *Die Freunde von Salamanca* ("The Friends from Salamanca"). A variety of virtuoso figuration decorates the tuneful line, and the movement concludes with a tranquil coda.

The vivacious Menuetto (movement V) develops in traditional three-part form with a gentle trio (Allegretto) intervening between its primary statements. The introduction to the sonata form finale (movement VI, F minor) offers a dramatic contrast—over an ominous tremolo cello line, the other players articulate forceful dotted figures until the momentum slows. The main part of the movement (F major) suggests a vigorous march. A fragment of the movement's introduction is reprised and the work concludes with a vibrant coda.

SIX

The Romantic Poet:
Schumann's Chamber Works

ROBERT SCHUMANN
B. JUNE 8, 1810 IN ZWICKAU, GERMANY,
D. JULY 29, 1856 IN ENDENICH, GERMANY

The intensely personal music of Robert Schumann represents for many listeners the epitome of Romanticism. His brief but productive life was marked by turbulent events that developed like brooding storms depicted in romantic painting. Vehement battles with Clara Wieck's father torturously delayed their eventual marriage; a self-induced hand injury painfully ended his career as a virtuoso pianist; mental disintegration preceded his death at the untimely age of 46. During most of his life, Schumann suffered from a disorder that he himself described as a split into several personalities. "More than one soul dwells within my breast," he confessed. By turns he became the impassioned, reckless "Florestan," the gentle, dreamy "Eusebius," or the rational "Raro." These diverse aspects of his temperament are continuously revealed in his music—mercurial contrasts of mood within movements reflect these distinctive personae that dominated his inner life. Unable to channel completely his protean musical ideas into established forms, Schumann created structures more flexible than had ever been heard in his era. Although grounded in classical principles, his fluent chamber compositions can be heard as romantic poems.

STRING QUARTETS

As an energetic youth, Robert Schumann embodied the romantic revolutionary. Essentially a self-taught composer, his musical goal was to liberate his art from classical bonds through his individual musical language that gained emotional resonance through literary associations. But after his marriage to the classically trained piano virtuoso Clara Wieck, he decided to immerse himself in close study of eighteenth-century string quartets and the counterpoint of Bach. Inspiration soon struck, and with fervor he wrote his three Opus 41 string quartets within five weeks in 1842. The set was dedicated to his colleague and friend, Felix Mendelssohn. The premiere of all three string quartets, his sole efforts in this demanding form, became a present to his beloved Clara on her twenty-third birthday. The quartets, he told her, were intended "to illuminate the depths of the human heart."

String Quartet in A Minor, Opus 41 No. 1

Introduzione: Andante espressivo—Allegro
Scherzo: Presto; Intermezzo
Adagio
Presto

Each of the four movements of the Opus 41 No. 1 Quartet develops with strong contrasts of mood, a reflection of Schumann's mercurial temperament. Despite its heightened emotional atmosphere, the quartet observes classical development principles, most importantly unity of conception. The key centers of A minor and F major anchor each movement, and the quartet achieves overall symmetry through similar thematic elements in the first movement and the finale.

Appended after the substantial sonata form Allegro section

(F major) had been completed, the quartet's introduction begins with imitative patterns inspired by Schumann's study of Bach. The elfin Scherzo (A minor), varied by the more sustained Intermezzo, suggests the fanciful influence of Mendelssohn. The songful Adagio (F major), the expressive center of the quartet, begins and concludes with a divinely soaring cello line. A thematic echo of the Adagio movement from Beethoven's Ninth Symphony heard at its center offers homage to the master. The exuberant Presto (A minor) develops with energetic figuration and dramatic upward leaps; it concludes with a jubilant coda in A major.

String Quartet in F Major, Opus 41 No. 2

Allegro vivace
Andante, quasi variazioni
Scherzo: Presto
Allegro molto vivace

The first of the string quartets to be composed, the Opus 41 No. 2 reveals Schumann's close study of Haydn and Beethoven. However, its warm lyricism suggests that Schumann's primary influence was Schubert. Earlier Schumann had written: "Schubert is my 'one and only' love, the more so as he has everything in common with my one and only Jean Paul." This revealing comment also suggests that the witty and fanciful novels by Johann Paul Friedrich Richter (1763–1825) were fully as influential for Schumann as his musical experiences.

The opening movement explores a primary theme, a rapturous song introduced by the violin, and a closely related second idea. This compact sonata form movement follows a straightforward development enlivened by energetic octave leaps that suggest "Florestan's" ebullience, a subtle scheme of dynamic markings and a brief harmonic excursion into the minor key.

The influence of Beethoven's slow movement from his Opus

127 quartet can be heard in the Opus 41 No. 2 second movement, "Slow, almost variations." Despite Schumann's word "almost" (which more accurately describes Beethoven's own Opus 127 movement), he crafted a true variation movement written as homage in the same A flat major key. Both develop with similarly syncopated metric patterns. Schumann, however, more persistently avoids barline pulses throughout the substantial variations 1, 4, and 5. Through subtle rhythmic manipulations he conjures an atmosphere of romantic ineffability.

The rapid and mysterious Scherzo (C minor) continues the metric displacements heard in the previous movement. Its trio section (C major) offers a low and sustained cello statement that suggests the rational verbal commentary of his inner "Raro" voice.

The Allegro molto vivace finale (F major) develops with dynamic upward leaping intervals and animated scale passages that suggest the impassioned voice of "Florestan." It concludes with a densely structured and accelerated coda.

String Quartet in A Major, Opus 41 No. 3

Andante espressivo: Allegro molto moderato
Assai agitato—Un poco adagio—Tempo risoluto
Adagio molto
Finale: Allegro molto vivace

Despite its formal flexibility, Quartet No. 3, like its predecessors in the set, is formally grounded by classical principles of sonata development. The quartet opens with a reflective introduction followed by two ardent themes—a warmly lyrical motif for the violin and a songful cello passage subtly animated by syncopated accompanying rhythms. Expressive changes of tempo articulate the movement's sonata form structure. The movement concludes with a softly descending interval in the cello that emulates a romantic sigh of the name "Clara."

The bold Assai agitato (F sharp minor) explores a restless subject through four variations energized by dramatic changes of meter; a quiet coda concludes the movement. The profound Adagio molto (D major), marked "always expressive," freely develops two rhapsodic themes. Eloquent viola statements suggest the lyrical influence of Mendelssohn's *Songs Without Words*. Energetic dotted figuration propels the powerful rondo finale (A major); a graceful trio section (F major) falls at its center. An extended coda drives the work to an exultant conclusion.

WORKS WITH VARIED SCORING

Piano Trio in F Major, Opus 80

Sehr lebhaft
Mit innigem Ausdruck—Lebhaft
In mässiger Bewegung
Nicht zu rasch

Although audiences have favored the first of Schumann's four piano trios, he himself preferred his more extroverted second trio in F major, Opus 80. He wrote to his friend Reinecke that "it made a quicker and more ingratiating appeal than the first," and that he found the beginning of the slow movement and the following Allegro to be quite successful. Written in 1847, Opus 80 develops with contrapuntal passages that reflect Schumann's recent study of J.S. Bach. Schumann composed the warmly romantic Opus 80 for his pianist wife Clara, who wrote: "This work touches my heart. I could go on playing it forever!"

The trio's opening movement, "Very lively," develops its three themes in freely rhapsodic sonata form. The second theme closely resembles the theme of his early song *Dein Bildnis wunderselig* ("Your wondrous blessed image"), Opus 39 No. 2. The introspective slow movement, "With inward expression," develops as a sustained lyric poem. Its two themes evolve through rich harmonies that progress from D flat major to A major, then A flat in its middle section ("Livelier") and return with intriguing excursions to the original key. The strings sing the main theme against piano figuration; the piano prevails in the more chromatic middle section.

The third movement, "With moderate movement" (B flat minor) is a graceful and somewhat wistful intermezzo. The three instruments imitatively develop the main theme, an idea energized by dotted rhythms. In its central section the piano develops a flowing theme; after a return of the opening material, the movement concludes with a brief coda. The ingenious finale, "Not too fast" (F major), develops two themes contrapuntally.

Piano Trio in G Minor, Opus 110

Bewegt, doch nicht zu rasch
Ziemlich langsam
Rasch
Kräftig, mit Humor

Schumann wrote his Opus 110 (1851) during his tenure as music director at Düsseldorf, a period when he created much chamber music for the available ensembles. Because Schumann was then preoccupied with effects of sonority and tone color, Opus 110 unfolds with unusual and radiant textures. Sudden changes of mood, also characteristic of Schumann's other three piano trios, abound.

The opening movement, "Moving but not too quick," explores two ideas, an undulating chord motive and a theme characterized by expressive leaps. The brief development leads into remote harmonic areas. The second movement, "Moderately slow," proceeds in a metrically intricate, three-part song form (E flat major).

The C minor scherzo movement, "Quick," is varied by a slower central section in C major. The finale, "Vigorous, with humor," is constructed as a mosaic of themes that collectively create a loose sonata form. The heroic second theme resembles Schumann's own favorite ballad, "The Two Grenadiers."

Piano Quartet in E flat Major, Opus 47

Sostenuto assai—Allegro ma non troppo
Scherzo: Molto vivace
Andante cantabile
Finale: Vivace

Schumann wrote his only piano quartet (1842) for Count Matvei Wielhorsky, an accomplished amateur cellist (and owner of a Golden Age Stradivarius) who performed at the work's premiere. The cello is featured in eloquent solo moments, particularly in the songful third movement. The opulent piano part of this warmly romantic work was intended for the virtuoso Clara.

As he composed his Opus 47, Schumann closely studied the chamber music of Haydn and Mozart and listened attentively to the masterly scherzos of his friend Mendelssohn. Classical influence is heard in the opening movement, a spacious sonata form with dramatic climactic moments. The fleet G minor Scherzo, extended by a second trio section, is unified by a recurrent staccato figure. The Andante cantabile, a yearning three-part song heard first in the cello, develops with unusual harmonies—most notably the key shift from B flat major to G flat major at its center. Near the conclusion the cellist must lower his string from C to B flat to play the final pedal chord. The Andante cantabile's last three notes relate to the primary theme of the exhilarating Vivace, an intricate movement with energetic fugal sections and lyrical passages juxtaposed.

Piano Quintet in E flat Major, Opus 44

Allegro brillante
In modo d'una marcia: Un poco largamente
Scherzo: Molto vivace
Allegro ma non troppo

Early in his career, Schumann often crafted groups of works in specific genres during intense binges of writing. In 1840, the year of his marriage to Clara Wieck against the vehement protests of her father, he created over 100 songs. The following year was devoted to symphonies. In 1842, guided by an inner voice that advised him to write chamber works, he created his three string quartets and his Opus 44 Piano Quintet. Written in the fervent heat of inspiration, the creation of these works exhausted Schumann. Shortly after their completion, he suffered the first of his mental breakdowns. Clara attributed his collapse to overwork and arranged for a stay at a Bohemian spa. However, he remained in fragile mental health for the duration of his brief life.

Schumann's Opus 44 Piano Quintet is regarded as one of the finest creations of 1842, his "chamber music year." At the time he composed these chamber works, he closely studied the compositional techniques of Haydn and Mozart—thus the intensely emotional and romantic Quintet develops formally according to an established classical design. The Quintet was dedicated to Clara, who expected to play its substantial piano part at the premiere. However, she fell ill, and Schumann's friend and colleague Felix Mendelssohn performed in her place. He subsequently suggested revisions, to which Schumann agreed. Robert even replaced a substantial part of his third movement with livelier "Mendelssohnian" themes.

Because the Quintet was written for the virtuoso Clara, it features a massive piano part and a broadly orchestral string score that provides a counterbalance. The work opens with a bold statement of the principal theme—a clearly profiled motif that recurs throughout the movement and again at the coda of the finale as a unifying device for the entire composition. The second theme is a reflective dialogue between the viola and cello. Both themes undergo a classically formal development, lavishly ornamented with virtuoso piano runs, and a recapitulation of ideas.

The somber character of the opening movement's second theme pervades the Un poco largamente (C minor). Described by Schumann as written "in the style of a march," the movement conjures a stately procession. Strongly contrasting lyrical and dramatic episodes are interspersed between statements of the main theme, presented by the first violin after a brief piano introduction.

The Scherzo opens with an E flat major scale pattern that is varied and repeated by all instruments. It offers two contrasting trio sections, the first of which explores a contemplative theme; the second trio inverts this melody, now accompanied by rapid figuration.

The robust finale develops both an emphatic motif, "always strongly marked," and a quieter second theme. As a departure from tradition, the movement opens in C minor and reaches its tonic key of E flat only after the third statement of the main theme. The remarkable coda introduces two fugal sections, each recapitulating elements heard earlier in the work.

CLARA SCHUMANN
B. SEPT. 13, 1819 IN LEIPZIG,
D. MAY 20, 1896 IN FRANKFURT

Piano Trio in G Minor, Opus 17

Allegro moderato
Scherzo: Tempo di Menuetto
Andante
Allegretto

By age fifteen German pianist and composer Clara Wieck was acclaimed throughout Europe as a phenomenally talented child prodigy. In 1840 she married Robert Schumann, and within eight years she bore eight children, seven of whom survived. Although she suffered severe time constraints during this period, especially since Robert could not be disturbed as he composed, she continued to concertize extensively, teach, and compose piano and chamber works—including her Opus 17 Trio.

Mendelssohn most probably inspired Clara's G Minor Piano Trio, her only chamber work, since the romantic atmosphere of its first and third movements suggests his ineffable *Songs Without Words*. Playful elements heard in the Scherzo evoke Felix's own delightful scherzi, much admired by Robert as well as Clara; a dramatic trio section provides contrast. The finale, based on a chromatic theme, develops with assured elegance. Written in 1846–1847 shortly before Robert created his own piano trios, the work unfolds with a wealth of flowing melodies, vivid harmonies, and a fine sense of craftsmanship. The trio was published in 1847.

Despite her creative abilities, Clara never had serious ambitions as a composer, most probably because nineteenth-century Germany was hostile to such aspirations in women. She entered in her diary in 1839: "I once thought that I possessed creative talent, but I have given up this idea. A woman must not desire to compose—not one has been able to do it, and why should I expect to? It would be arrogance, although indeed my father led me into it in earlier days."

It has been thought that the final compositions of Robert Schumann reveal the hand of Clara. As he became incapacitated by his mental illness, she most probably helped to guide and refine his musical thoughts.

SEVEN

A Prodigy's Progress:
Mendelssohn's Chamber Works

FELIX MENDELSSOHN
B. FEB. 3, 1809 IN HAMBURG,
D. NOV. 4, 1847 IN LEIPZIG

During his lifetime Felix Mendelssohn was honored in his native Germany as "the Mozart of the Nineteenth Century" (a term coined by his friend Robert Schumann), and he was lauded as a phenomenal genius throughout Europe. One of the greatest conductors of his generation and an outstanding performer of both piano and violin, Mendelssohn above all else was a prolific composer in a variety of genres. A Romantic who remained faithful to earlier structural concepts, Mendelssohn created twelve classically-proportioned chamber works fired by his lyrical imagination. All are staples of the repertoire.

Mendelssohn's strong work ethic was instilled at an early age by his wealthy, highly achieving family. When he was a young child his parents normally woke him before dawn to begin a long day of tutoring sessions in a wide range of subjects, including painting and gymnastics. Mendelssohn spoke of his formidable work habits in an interview with one of his composition students: "If I am considered to have originality, I realize that I owe most of that to my strict self-criticism and my drive to change and better myself. I have turned and tested my ideas—how frequently I altered each one!—in order to transform their ordinary physiognomy into a more original, more meaningful and effective one. Give me an idea of the most ordinary kind and you may wager that I will turn and twist it in shape through instrumentation, harmony, and accompaniment to make it a decent piece." He added, with a touch of modesty: "One must put a little trust in luck too."

STRING QUARTETS

String Quartet in E flat Major, Opus 12

Adagio non troppo—Allegro non tardante
Canzonetta: Allegretto
Andante espressivo
Molto allegro e vivace

Of the six string quartets composed by Felix Mendelssohn, the early Opus 12 has proved to be his most popular. After his graduation from the University of Berlin, Mendelssohn sailed to England in 1829. He soon wrote to his sister Fanny: "My quartet is now in the middle of the last movement, and I think it will be completed in a few days." Although he was only twenty years old, Mendelssohn had already acquired fluency in quartet composition. The first of his string quartets to be published, the Opus 12 was actually written two years after his brilliant adolescent quartet, the Opus 13.

A brief and restrained introduction, distinguished by a rising three-note motto theme, precedes the main section of the first movement. The first theme is an expansive, singing melody that gradually becomes subdued; the calmer second theme follows the same rhythmic pattern as the first. After development of these ideas, a pensive new theme is heard in the second violin, accompanied by the viola. The themes are recapitulated in a poised and poetic atmosphere.

As a departure from the traditional scherzo, the second movement is inspired by the sixteenth-century canzonetta, a light and dancelike song. Particularly favored as an encore movement, this graceful canzonetta enlivens its ideas with effective staccato and pizzicato passages. In its central section there is a charming exchange between the two violins over pedal tones in the viola and cello.

The three-note motto heard at the introduction to the first movement forms the basis of the Andante espressivo's noble theme. An improvisatory recitative for the first violin, marked "with fire," leads to an embellished restatement of the opening material.

Proceeding without pause, the finale opens with two emphatic chords. The movement resembles a tarantella, a demonically rapid dance that was once believed to cure tarantula bite. At its midpoint, the viola plays a reprise of the pensive theme from the first movement. The vivacious mood returns, and the work concludes with a coda based on themes from the opening movement.

String Quartet in A Minor, Opus 13

Adagio—Allegro vivace
Adagio non lento
Intermezzo: Allegretto con moto—Allegro di molto
Presto—Adagio non lento

Mendelssohn began his Opus 13 Quartet (1827), the first of his six string quartets, when he was an eighteen-year-old infatuated with a young woman he had met during a family summer sojourn in the Harz Mountains. His boyhood friend Johann Gustav Droysen had recently written a poem entitled *Ist es wahr?* ("Is it True?") and Mendelssohn thought its opening line, "Is it true that you always wait for me in the arbor?" reflected his own intense feelings. Mendelssohn set Droysen's entire poem in his Opus 9 No. 1 song, which is often performed as a prelude to Opus 13. The song's opening three-note phrase becomes a motto that pervades the entire quartet. Like a secret program, it is sometimes quoted directly, but more often it is heard as an echo through similar rhythms and intervals.

Opus 13 can also be heard as an homage to Beethoven, who died soon after Mendelssohn began his quartet. The work reveals his thorough knowledge of Beethoven's late quartets—particularly Opus 132, which inspired the work's finale. Fugal treatment heard in Beethoven's Opus 95 slow movement appears similarly in Mendelssohn's Adagio. Like Beethoven, Mendelssohn unifies the quartet's structure by interweaving thematic connections between the movements.

The quartet begins with a slow introduction (A major) that clearly states the motto, identifiable by its long-short-long rhythmic pattern. The Allegro vivace (A minor) then surges ahead with a statement of two impassioned themes. After the development—energized by ingenious counterpoint and subtle dissonance—and a free recapitulation of ideas, the movement concludes with a forceful coda.

The Adagio opens with a paraphrase of Mendelssohn's original song. The viola then states a second theme, which is treated fugally in the manner of Beethoven. An ardent violin cadenza leads to a reprise of the opening section.

The Allegretto con moto that frames the graceful three-part Intermezzo offers a haunting first violin solo lightly accompanied by the other strings. The rapid and delicate middle section, Allegro di molto, suggests his Overture to *A Midsummer Night's Dream,* composed when he was seventeen years old.

Essentially an homage to Beethoven's Opus 132 Quartet, the Presto begins with a dramatic violin recitative that recalls its introduction to the finale. As the movement develops, motifs from Opus 13's earlier movements and its *Ist es wahr?* motto are interjected.

The movement concludes with a serene restatement of the poem's original setting.

String Quartet in D Major, Opus 44 No. 1

Molto allegro vivace
Menuetto: Un poco allegretto
Andante espressivo ma con moto
Presto con brio

Mendelssohn wrote the three quartets comprising his Opus 44 set in 1837–38, a time of personal contentment for this incessant worker. Happily married and recently the father of a son, Mendelssohn basked in his secure international reputation. Because he followed an arduous touring schedule, Mendelssohn composed primarily during the relatively calm summer months. He completed Opus 44 No. 1, the final quartet of the set despite its listing, in late July 1838 and dedicated it to the Crown Prince of Sweden. He indicated in a letter to a friend that this quartet was his favorite of the set: "I have just finished my third quartet, in D major, and I like it very much. It is more spirited than the others and seems to me to be more congenial for the players."

The opening movement develops two themes, the first spirited and exuberant, the second more restrained. A compact recapitulation leads into the vibrant coda. As a contrast to this energetic movement, Mendelssohn replaced his characteristic rapid scherzo movement with the more tranquil Menuetto (D major); its haunting central section (B minor) reiterates flowing eighth note patterns. The reflective Andante movement (B minor) develops two lyrical themes in sonata form. The finale resembles a brilliant *saltarello*, a lively Italian dance. As in the preceding movements, two contrasting themes are developed. High spirits and virtuosic passagework drive the movement to an exuberant conclusion.

String Quartet in E Minor, Opus 44 No. 2

Allegro assai appassionato
Scherzo: Allegro di molto
Andante
Presto agitato

Mendelssohn composed his Opus 44 No. 2 in July 1837 while enjoying an extended honeymoon with his bride Cécile, who painted watercolors as Felix composed. The E Minor Quartet was the first of his Opus 44 set to be written but was the second to be published.

Mendelssohn's friend Robert Schumann commented on the classical serenity that pervades his colleague's music of the late 1830s: "A smile hovers around his mouth, but it is that of delight in his art, of quiet self-sufficiency in an intimate circle." Smooth construction and exquisite balance characterize each of the Opus 44 quartets.

The Allegro assai appassionato opens with two primary motifs—a calm theme in the violin that is energized by syncopations in the second violin and viola, followed by a lyrical theme in the first violin accompanied by contrapuntal lines in the other instruments. The cello introduces a third idea in its songful upper register. After a development and recapitulation of ideas, the movement concludes with a powerful coda that incorporates the two main themes.

The delicate Scherzo (E major) is based on a distinctive rhythmic figure consisting of repeated staccato notes. The contrasting middle section develops with playful asymmetry. Here the viola introduces a melodious theme that is repeated near the end of this graceful movement.

An ardent declaration of warm emotion, the Andante (G major) recalls Mendelssohn's *Songs Without Words*, piano works commenced in 1829. This three-part movement begins with a songful melody in the violin accompanied by flowing passages in the other voices. A second theme is introduced in the more agitated middle section. After a brief development of the new idea, the passionate mood returns as the cello sings the opening theme.

The Presto finale (E minor) is a perpetuum mobile with two themes—a vivacious dance melody and a melodious song. The two ideas are combined throughout the movement, but the dancelike motif predominates at the energetic conclusion.

String Quartet in F Minor, Opus 80

Allegro vivace assai
Allegro assai
Adagio
Finale: Allegro molto

One of Mendelssohn's few autobiographical works, the Opus 80 string quartet expresses his grief over the death of his beloved sister Fanny, a gifted musician and a constant source of inspiration for him. In May 1847 Mendelssohn returned from a successful but exhausting trip to England, where he had conducted numerous performances of his recently revised oratorio Elijah. Two days later Fanny, in apparent good health, died suddenly of a stroke; she was only 41. "God help us all!" Mendelssohn wrote. "I've been incapable of saying or thinking anything beyond that. For many days to come, I'll be unable to write anything beyond—God help us, God help us!" On the opening page of his Opus 80 Mendelssohn inscribed the initials of this phrase in German, *Hilf Du mir*.

Mendelssohn himself would live only another year, one that was marred by constant infirmities. In the summer of 1847 he and his wife Cécile travelled to Interlaken, Switzerland with hopes that he would recuperate. There he completed a working draft of his Opus 80 and that October, a month before his death, premiered the work at his home. A friend wrote after this occasion: "The passionate character of the entire piece seems to me to be consistent with his deeply disturbed frame of mind. He is still grappling with grief at the loss of his sister." The quartet was published posthumously in 1850.

Before he allowed a work to be published, Mendelssohn customarily made extensive revisions during the proofreading stage. ("It's my habit and there's no cure for it," he wrote in apology to his publisher.) Since Mendelssohn died before he could review the work in a publishing context, one might conclude that Opus 80 had not reached its definitive form for Mendelssohn. Possible thematic and developmental omissions are most evident in the quartet's stark finale. However, the structural simplicity of this movement and the reiterations of its opening idea recall his fervent repetitions of "God help us!"

Profound emotion characterizes each of the quartet's four movements, three of which are related by their F minor key structure. The sonorous opening movement, in sonata form, develops two themes that are propelled by energetic figures in the accompanying voices. The movement concludes with an agitated coda (Presto).

The Allegro assai is Mendelssohn's most poignant scherzo. Its syncopated theme, heard first in the violin, moves with persistent accents that suggest agitation. The sustained Adagio (A flat major) recalls Mendelssohn's earlier *Songs without Words*. Wide dynamic ranges contribute to the emotional intensity.

The fervent F minor Finale develops two restless themes in sonata form. Tremolo passagework in the accompanying voices intensifies its implicit anguish. The movement concludes with an impassioned high-register statement in which the first violin declaims its opening motto in a fortissimo dynamic.

WORKS WITH VARIED SCORING

Piano Trio in D Minor, Opus 49

Molto allegro agitato
Andante con moto tranquillo
Scherzo: Leggiero e vivace
Finale: Allegro assai appassionato

Mendelssohn's Piano Trio in D Minor achieved immediate popular success, in part because composer and music critic Robert Schumann described it as "the master trio of the age, as were the trios of Beethoven and Schubert in their times." A challenge for the pianist, the keyboard writing is virtuoso throughout; Mendelssohn deliberately incorporated technically challenging keyboard figuration characteristic of Liszt and Chopin into the keyboard score. Yet the piano does not dominate the texture, which remains translucent, and the trio's classical structure is always evident despite its romantically florid figuration.

The first movement develops two radiant themes in sonata form. Both are introduced by the cello in its deeply songful middle range and explored by all instruments. The lyrical second movement, which recalls his *Songs Without Words*, falls into three parts: a statement of the theme in the piano; a contrasting minor-key section; a variation of the opening section. The elfin Scherzo is a technically challenging whirlwind that varies its central theme with charmingly contrasting episodes. The Finale, rhythmically based on the poetic foot of the dactyl (one long accented beat followed by two short beats), is a tour de force that brings the work to an exhilarating conclusion.

String Quintet in B flat Major, Opus 87

Allegro vivace
Andante scherzando
Adagio e lento
Allegro molto vivace

Mendelssohn completed his Opus 87, the second of his two string quintets, in the summer of 1845, a serene time during which he also worked on his oratorio Elijah. The B flat Quintet was published posthumously in 1851, leading to speculation that Mendelssohn had possibly planned revisions.

The Opus 87 radiates serene lyricism throughout. The Allegro vivace explores two themes, an energetic first subject based on a triadic figure and a songful second idea. After full development of these themes, a fiery buildup leads to a recapitulation of the opening ideas. The substantial coda develops the themes further through contrapuntal treatment.

A graceful scherzo, the Andante scherzando (G minor) departs from the elfin dances traditionally associated with Mendelssohn's inner movements. Fugal passages and shifting accents lend piquancy to its elegant cantabile melodies.

The third movement (D minor) is a slow elegy that opens with a theme of great pathos. Poignantly expressive harmonies fluctuate between major and minor. At the climactic moment, orchestral in conception, the elegiac theme resembles an impassioned rhapsody. The movement closes with dramatic tremolos that lead directly to the finale.

Rhythmically varied and richly syncopated, the Allegro molto vivace develops two themes in modified classical sonata form. The energetic counterpoint of this good-natured movement recalls Mendelssohn's popular String Octet, written twenty years earlier.

Sextet in D Major for Piano and Strings, Opus 110

Allegro vivace
Adagio
Menuetto: Agitato
Allegro vivace

Mendelssohn wrote his brilliant Sextet for Piano and Strings over the course of thirteen days in 1824 when he was fifteen years old. The work was published posthumously in 1868 as Opus 110 (a misleadingly high opus number that refers to order of publication rather than order of composition). During his early adolescence Felix intently studied the scores of a variety of significant composers—Weber, Mozart, and Beethoven, among others—and experimented with their techniques in his own compositions. His family provided strong motivation for him to compose prolifically. Their large Berlin estate provided the setting for weekly Sunday morning musicales at which the most distinguished musicians of the day concertized informally. A capable pianist, violinist, and violist, Felix performed on whatever instrument was needed for presentation of his latest works. He absorbed the musical suggestions that followed these sessions and blossomed as a composer.

The spirited virtuoso style of the Sextet suggests the influence of Carl Maria von Weber, an early Mendelssohn favorite. Like Weber, long stretches of the two Allegro vivace movements are scored with high decorative runs in the piano over supportive bass progressions.

The opening Allegro vivace movement explores its two themes in classical sonata form. Its clear development, recapitulation, and effervescent coda section contribute to a crystalline effect. The serene Adagio opens with a gentle melody in the muted strings; the piano offers a reply. The piano and strings exchange their reflective material throughout, and the movement reaches a quiet conclusion. The emphatic Menuetto is a demonic scherzo in D minor; its major key trio section provides a smoother contrast.

Octet in E flat Major for Strings, Opus 20

Allegro moderato con fuoco
Andante
Scherzo: Allegro leggierissimo
Presto

The sixteen-year-old Mendelssohn wrote his Octet during the summer and fall of 1825. Considered to be the most outstanding chamber composition ever written by one so young, the Octet honored the 23rd birthday of Eduard Rietz, Mendelssohn's violin teacher. It premiered to great acclaim at one of the weekly Mendelssohn family musicales.

In his Octet Mendelssohn, who had been composing for only five years, achieved his own unique idiom, one that develops romantic ideas within a classical framework. All four movements follow sonata form, the established eighteenth-century framework heard in the works of the great classicists. Yet Mendelssohn succeeds in conjuring a romantic landscape, particularly in the fanciful scherzo movement.

The first movement develops two themes, a soaring motif in the first violin and a more lyrical theme heard first as a violin and viola duet. Tremolos and syncopations contribute to the rich, orchestral texture. After a development and recapitulation that offers intriguing variants of the ideas, a fiery coda concludes the movement. The serene Andante, moving in a lilting *siciliano* rhythm, varies its folklike themes with animated interweaving of the motifs.

The magical Scherzo is the romantic highlight of the Octet. Mendelssohn is believed to have been inspired by a passage from Goethe's *Faust*: "Trails of cloud and mist brighten from above; breezes in the foliage and wind in the reeds—everything is scattered." Mendelssohn's sister Fanny explains the movement: "It must be played staccato and pianissimo. All is new and strange

... one feels near a world of ghosts, lightly blown aloft. At the end the first violin flutters upward, light as a feather—and all vanishes away." The Scherzo theme returns, together with new ideas, in the eight-part fugato of the finale.

EIGHT

The Nostalgic Romanticist: Brahms's Chamber Works

JOHANNES BRAHMS
B. MAY 7, 1833 IN HAMBURG,
D. APRIL 3, 1897 IN VIENNA

To his adoring Viennese audiences Brahms stood as Beethoven's heir, an honor that the relentlessly self-critical Johannes considered a burden: "One will never know how it feels to have the tramp of a giant like Beethoven behind him," he wrote. Reluctant to have his own chamber works compared to Beethoven's undisputed master-pieces, Brahms composed his quartets and trios with the utmost deliberation. Moreover, he burned any work that did not meet his lofty standards. In contrast to the hundreds of songs that flowed easily from his pen, Brahms produced only three string quartets over the course of his long career—but he admitted to destroying at least twenty quartets in various stages of development.

During Brahms's lifetime, the influential cultural critic and philosopher Friedrich Nietzsche (1844–1900) derided him as a composer of the past—a criticism that ignored Brahms's towering achievement of summarizing a vast sweep of musical developments. Brahms admired older music, and he frequently incorporated Bach's counterpoint as well as occasional rhythmic gestures from the medieval era into his works. He channeled Mozart's Classi-cism and Schubert's lyrical Romanticism. But Brahms's primary influence was Beethoven, and he sought to construct works according to his masterful principles. Ironically, it was Brahms's obsession with Beethoven's techniques that endeared him to the great twentieth-century pioneer Arnold Schoenberg. This champion of the twelve-tone system, also a Viennese, heard a kindred spirit in Brahms's technique of "developing variation," whereby small motifs are relentlessly expanded and manipulated to create a large and coherent structure. In his essay "Brahms the Progressive" (1947) Schoenberg proclaimed Brahms a like-minded modernist.

Brahms's genius perhaps lies in the strength of his melodic invention. Like Schubert, Brahms composed lyrical themes with spontaneity. In contrast to his densely written sonata form movements, strongly influenced by the Classicists, the slow movements of his chamber works develop freely as warm, extended songs that place him among the true Romantics.

CHAMBER WORKS FOR STRINGS

String Quartet in C Minor, Opus 51 No. 1

Allegro
Romanze: Poco Adagio
Allegretto molto moderato e comodo
Allegro

As early as 1855 Brahms's violinist friend Joseph Joachim inquired how the C Minor Quartet was progressing. Fourteen years later Brahms sent Clara Schumann its two outer movements before deciding that they were not yet ready for public hearing. The premiere of his first quartet, the Opus 51 No. 1, finally occurred in

1873 after two full decades of revising and polishing. The work was dedicated to his physician friend Theodor Billroth since, as Brahms stated in a letter, he "needed a doctor for its difficult birth."

Heroic and defiant, the Opus 51 No. 1 reveals a profundity that is typical of works by both Brahms and Beethoven in the key of C minor. The three strongly-profiled themes of the sonata form opening Allegro are developed with logic and concentration that suggest the influence of Beethoven's later string quartets, particularly his rugged Opus 95 "Serioso." Alternately soft and loud thematic fragments punctuate the development, harmonically organized as A minor-E major-C minor. The substantial coda, marked "increasing in dynamics and agitated" echoes the powerful endings of Beethoven's own works. The Romanze (A flat major), cast in three-part song form, recalls Beethoven in its pensive and expressive middle section, in which some listeners hear a suggestion of the Cavatina from Beethoven's late Opus 130 quartet.

The multi-sectioned third movement opens with a restless F minor statement animated by displaced accents; a graceful interlude (A flat major) precedes the return of the opening material. The trio section (F major) suggests a Viennese waltz accompanied by leisurely pizzicato figures in the cello. The tempestuous Allegro finale (C minor) resembles the opening movement in its vehemence. Its three themes are developed in A-B-A song form; the rhythmically animated central section is cast in C major. The movement concludes with an extended C minor coda marked "stringendo," or gradually increasing in speed.

String Quartet in A Minor, Opus 51 No. 2

Allegro non troppo
Andante moderato
Quasi Minuetto, moderato—Allegro vivace
Finale: Allegro non assai

The String Quartet in A Minor was premiered and dedicated to Brahms's physician friend Theodor Billroth in 1873 after eighteen years of revising and polishing. Although Brahms was a fine violist, he nevertheless constantly sought the advice of his violinist friend Joachim when composing for strings. The lyrically intense Quartet No. 2 pays homage to this indispensable colleague, whose personal motto was *Frei, aber einsam* ("Free, but lonely"). The notes F-A-E form the main part of the first movement's elegiac main theme and are woven into the texture throughout the work. Brahms also interpolates his own motto, *Frei, aber froh* ("Free, but glad"), interpreted musically as the notes F-A-F. The development section of the first movement, a tour de force of contrapuntal writing, exploits these two mottos through canons, inversions, and retrograde motion.

The Andante of Opus 51 No. 2, written in three-part song form, opens with a warm theme in A major ("expressive and smooth"). A tempestuous section with jagged rhythms (F sharp minor, "strongly marked") enters abruptly. After a calmer transition section (F major) the sinuous opening theme returns with variations.

The Quasi Minuetto ("almost a minuet," A minor) develops with graceful charm despite its complex contrapuntal writing. Double canons and rhythmically subtle passages of imitation abound in this A-B-A form movement. A humorous moment occurs in the faster midsection ("light and vivacious," A major) where an imitative passage combined with sly syncopations in all instruments gives the impression of a musical chase. A similar moment of Brahms's levity is heard in the rondo finale, which resembles a vibrant Hungarian dance. The cello, playing on the beat, briefly appears to have fallen behind his companions, who play in syncopation with him. At the coda the opening theme of the first movement is heard in canon between the cello and first violin. The tempo accelerates dramatically as the other instruments join.

String Quartet in B flat Major, Opus 67 ("The Hunt")

Vivace
Andante
Agitato (Allegretto non troppo)
Poco Allegretto con Variazioni

Although each of Brahms's three surviving quartets was published within the narrow window of 1873–75, he had refined and polished their movements for over two decades. Brahms completed Opus 67, the third and final quartet of the set, during the last stages of composing his First Symphony (a fourteen-year project). Possibly a welcome respite from these ardors, the quartet strikes a joyous spirit at the outset—the opening melody suggests a vigorous hunting fanfare. Like Mozart's eponymous K. 458 "Hunt" Quartet in B flat, "The Hunt" has also become a popular nickname for Brahms's quartet. Brahms initially described the work as a "trifle" but later admitted it was the favorite of his string quartets.

The exuberant Vivace derives much of its energy from both unexpected accents and the juxtaposition of differing rhythms. Its three contrasting themes are developed in sonata form; a brilliant coda based on the hunting theme concludes the movement. The Andante (F major) is cast in three-part song form. At its center, the serene opening melody is interrupted by emphatic, declamatory chords and terse rhythms. After a ritardando, the cello brings a return of the opening idea in a passage marked "sweet and graceful." Subtle syncopations energize the tranquil conclusion.

Brahms described the D minor Agitato (enigmatically notated "moderately allegro but not too much") as "the most tender and

most impassioned movement I have ever written." A complex intermezzo—for Brahms a poetic statement in a moderate tempo—the
movement requires all strings to be muted except the viola, which
articulates its fervent themes with urgency. A central trio section
(A minor) offers a flowing contrast. The opening material returns
and the movement concludes with a pianissimo coda.

Based on an insouciant theme, the finale (B flat major) offers
eight variations with conversational exchanges among the players.
After an excursion into the remote key of G flat major (six flat keys),
the hunting fanfare motif developed in the first movement returns
at the seventh variation. A soft and sinuous passage in B flat minor
leads to an assertive coda (B flat major) that combines the finale's
opening theme with the hunting fanfare.

String Quintet in F Major, Opus 88 ("Spring")

Allegro non troppo ma con brio
Grave ed appassionato—Allegretto vivace—Presto
Allegro energico—Presto

Written with unusual speed during the peak of his creative
life, Brahms expressed rare satisfaction with his Opus 88 Quintet
(1882). He wrote to his publisher: "I can tell you that you have
not as yet had such a beautiful work from me, and probably you
have not published one such in the last ten years." (Ironically, Opus
88 is perhaps the least performed of all Brahms's chamber works.)
Often called the "Spring" Quintet, Opus 88 was completed at the
Austrian resort of Bad Ischl, where he enjoyed fine weather and the
company of his composer friend Ignaz Brüll, his favorite partner in
four-hands piano works.

Opus 88 opens with an amiable, richly harmonized theme that
suggests the later songs of Schubert; the influence of Schubert can
also be heard in harmonic relationships that echo the ethereal
progressions of his 1826 C Major Cello Quintet. The first viola

offers the lyrical second theme as the other instruments introduce intricate counter-rhythms. The development explores the two ideas through inventive counterpoint.

The F Major Quintet combines both the traditional slow movement and scherzo in its central rondo, marked "Solemn and passionate" then "fast and lively." These contrasting sections alternate with variations three times throughout. The themes are based on two of Brahms's unpublished neo-baroque piano works from 1858—the slow section was borrowed from his A Major Sarabande and the rapid interludes from his A Major Gavotte. The affecting (Neapolitan) harmonic inflections at the end perhaps influenced Dvořák's haunting New World Symphony Largo introduction ten years later.

The Allegro energico reveals the influence of Beethoven's Rasumovsky Quartet Opus 59 No. 3—both quartet finales are fugal sonata form movements that begin with a solo viola statement. The movement develops with virtuoso contrapuntal passages throughout. The triple-time dancelike Presto functions as an extended coda; the passage gradually increases its dynamic level and concludes with four emphatic F major chords.

String Quintet in G Major, Opus 111

Allegro non troppo, ma con brio
Adagio
Un poco Allegretto
Vivace ma non troppo presto

Brahms spent working summers at Bad Ischl, an idyllic resort in Austria's Lake Country, and Opus 111, his second quintet for two violas, resulted from his sojourn of 1890. Once back in Vienna, his friends were impressed by the "sunny country of the new quintet," as his student Elisabeth von Herzogenberg phrased it. "This surpasses your earlier works in beauty, grace, and depth of feeling," she enthused. "He who can invent all this must be in a happy frame of mind. It is the work of a man of 30!" At a rehearsal for the quintet's premiere later that season, a friend observed that the good-natured work should be subtitled "Brahms in the Prater," a reference to the composer's favorite Viennese park. Brahms gladly agreed: "Exactly right! Among all the pretty girls."

However, by the time Brahms submitted the work to his publisher, his mood had grown somber. Because the quintet incorporated sketches for a projected symphony that Brahms knew would remain incomplete, his discouragement was immense. He wrote: "With this letter you can bid farewell to my music, because it is high time to stop. The fact that you have gotten this quintet is due to a trick that my modesty has played on me." Fortunately, Brahms recovered his sense of mission as a composer and continued to write until nearly the end of his life.

The exuberant first movement is based on drafts that Brahms had sketched for his fifth symphony. It opens with symphonic fullness as the four upper strings vigorously play tremolo and the cello line rises heroically from beneath. The quieter second theme is a songful phrase for violas with rhythmic accompaniments in the violins and cello. A third theme, introduced by the first violin, resembles a charming Viennese waltz.

The concise and profound Adagio (D minor) is a set of variations on an intensely expressive theme heard initially in the violas. The theme is varied at each of its three statements to create a subtly different character.

The scherzo movement ("a little lively," G minor) opens with a pensive waltz tune. The middle section (G major) develops a dialogue between the violins and violas against arpeggiated figuration in the cello. After a return of the first section, the movement concludes with an introspective coda.

The violas introduce the Magyar-inspired theme of the Vivace finale, and the ensemble responds with a forceful statement. The first violin introduces an arpeggiated second theme. The

momentum builds and the movement concludes with an unin-
hibited Hungarian dance.

String Sextet in B flat Major, Opus 18

Allegro ma non troppo
Andante, ma moderato
Scherzo: Allegro molto
Rondo: Poco Allegretto e grazioso

In the autumn of 1857 Brahms accepted a part-time post at
the Court of Detmold, located in a picturesque castle set in a
German forest. His light duties at this tranquil backwater were
to instruct the young resident princess in piano and to perform at
court functions. Detmold became a haven for Brahms, then still
recovering from the death of his close friend Robert Schumann and
his unrequited love for Robert's wife Clara. Restored by his long
forest walks, he began several chamber works, among which was
the Opus 18 Sextet. Because of continuous polishing and lengthy
revisions, the work was completed and premiered three years later.

The first of Brahms's two string sextets, Opus 18 has been
described as romantic emotion bridled by classical form. The
influence of Beethoven and Haydn is heard consistently in the
work's supple motivic treatment and its clear presentation of
themes, always warmly conveyed with Brahms's uniquely romantic
intensity.

The Allegro ma non troppo develops three lyrical themes. The
first cello, prominent throughout the work, presents the singing
opening theme, and the first violin articulates the graceful second
idea. The entire ensemble offers the third theme, which resembles
an Austrian country dance. The Andante (D minor) is a set of six
variations and coda based on an unknown theme, an archaic melody
with a strongly profiled bass line. Brahms was so fond of this movement that he arranged the variations as a piano solo, which he often

performed for friends. The Scherzo (F major) unfolds with rustic humor suggesting Beethoven's scherzo movement from his *Pastoral Symphony*. The finale ("slightly fast and graceful") is a classically structured rondo that concludes with jubilance.

String Sextet in G Major, Opus 36

Allegro non troppo
Scherzo: Allegro non troppo—Presto giocoso
Poco Adagio
Poco Allegro

In 1858 Brahms met and fell in love with Agathe von Siebold, a professor's daughter and an accomplished singer. The following year he exchanged rings with her. But when a friend suggested that he should proceed with the promised wedding, Brahms panicked. He wrote to Agathe: "I love you! I must see you again, but I cannot wear fetters! Write me whether I may come back to fold you in my arms, to tell you that I love you!" Agathe refused to see him. Feeling much compromised, she left for Ireland to become a governess.

Years after their relationship had ended, Brahms continued to feel remorse for his scandalous behavior. To ease his conscience, he wrote the second of his two string sextets for Agathe and wove the musical spelling of her name into the music. Omitting only the T, he crafted the second theme of the first movement out of the letters A-G-A-H (the note B in German usage)-E. After the Sextet was completed in 1864, Brahms wrote to a friend: "Here I have freed myself from my last love!"

The first violin plays the soaring opening theme of the Allegro non troppo, and the cello begins the ardent second theme. The music gains intensity, and the first violin and first viola forcefully articulate the "Agathe" theme three times. After extensive development of motives, the movement concludes with a reflective coda. The three-part second movement begins with a graceful theme based on a neo-baroque piano gavotte that Brahms had written ten years earlier. The trio section, written in a contrasting triple meter, suggests a rustic peasant dance. A condensed version of the opening Scherzo then returns.

The Poco Adagio is a set of five variations of a melody reminiscent of the Sextet's opening motive. Brahms based this theme on a sketch that he had sent to Clara Schumann, perhaps his deepest love, ten years earlier. The dancelike finale develops two contrasting themes and concludes with a vivacious coda.

PIANO TRIOS

Piano Trio in B Major, Opus 8

Allegro con brio
Scherzo: Allegro molto
Adagio
Allegro

An unusual history haunts Brahms's Opus 8 Piano Trio, the original of which exists in ghostly limbo. The trio premiered in two vastly different versions, the first in 1855 and the second in 1890. Before he reluctantly published his first version at the urging of Schumann and their mutual violinist friend Joachim, Brahms had already burned numerous piano trio efforts. Soon after its publication he pronounced the Opus 8 "wild" and regretted that he did not destroy it as well. While vacationing on Austria's River Traun thirty-seven years later, Brahms recalled that Clara Schumann had objected to the trio's many tempo changes. He then revisited the work and pared its length by a full third. Brahms deleted all thematic quotes from fellow Viennese composers—an elaborate and lengthy homage—and substantially recast three movements with new secondary themes. Only the Scherzo remained intact. Unfortunately, Brahms was also dissatisfied with his revised trio. He wrote to his publisher: "About the renewed trio, I must expressly state that while the old one is bad, I do not assert that the new one is good!" Musician friends received the revised trio with misgivings. "You have no right to impose your masterly touch on this loveable, if sometimes vague, product of your youth," wrote one. Despite all protests, Opus 8's attractive early version has rarely been performed since Brahms published his revision.

The second version of Opus 8 is distinguished by its rich and masterful development of gorgeous themes. Brahms's deep appreciation for Germany's vast trove of lyrical song, much of it folk, permeates the work. The radiant opening theme of the first movement, introduced by the piano and cello, became one of Brahms's admitted favorites. The piquant, staccato-phrased Scherzo ("very fast," B minor) is varied by a warmly songful trio section (B major); a quiet and whimsical coda concludes the movement. Cast as a three-part song, the Adagio's expressive center is a poignant cello statement developed in partnership with the violin. The cello introduces the restless opening theme of the finale, and the piano presents its forceful second theme, energized by syncopated accents in the cello. The coda, marked "a bit more animated," reaffirms the movement's opening idea.

Piano Trio in C Major, Opus 87

Allegro
Andante con moto
Scherzo: Presto
Finale: Allegro giocoso

Brahms began his Opus 87, the second of his three surviving trios for piano, violin, and cello, during his customary summer sojourn at the fashionable Bad Ischl spa resort. At its private home premiere in 1882 Brahms played one of his notorious practical jokes by introducing its pianist, Ignaz Brüll, as the actual composer of the trio. True authorship was quickly established, and the trio was praised as evidence that Brahms had reached a new peak of creativity.

The opening Allegro begins with an incisive motif in the violin and cello. Its theme groups, energetic and reflective by turns, are transformed and varied throughout. A recapitulation of ideas and an extensive coda conclude this sonata form movement.

The emotional center of the trio, the Andante con moto (A minor) offers five variations on a noble theme that is possibly of Hungarian origin. Heard initially in the violin and cello, this theme is dramatically recast into a heroic statement (third variation) to a joyous one (fourth variation, A major), then finally to an ethereal fifth statement (A minor). The mysterious Scherzo (C minor) is varied by its soaring and genial trio (C major); the shadows return with a repeat of the opening section.

Brahms described his exuberant finale as "giocoso" (playful). This sonata rondo movement develops two contrasting themes—a fervent idea heard initially in the strings, and a lighter second theme that exploits differing meters in all instruments.

Piano Trio in C Minor, Opus 101

Allegro energico
Presto non assai
Andante grazioso
Allegro molto

Variously described by his critics as "defiant, wild, and forceful to the verge of asperity" and as a work that "completely carried me away" by his special friend Clara Schumann, Brahms's final piano trio (1886) is a work of extraordinary power and concentration. Like much of his late chamber music, the trio expresses heightened Romanticism with an economy of gesture.

Comprised of four notes heard initially in piano octaves, the Allegro energico's primary motif recurs in varying guises throughout the trio. The expansive second idea (E flat major) is a songful passage for the strings. Constructed with keen rhythmic subtlety, the movement alternates between strongly marked rhythmic patterns and dovetailing phrases that disguise the metrical pulse.

In the Presto non assai ("fast but not too much," C minor), the strings are muted to create a spectral atmosphere. The piano introduces the second thematic area, marked "agitated" (F minor); the strings respond with piquant arpeggiation.

The Andante (C major) is based on a folklike theme that moves asymmetrically—one three-beat bar alternates with two two-beat bars to create a seven-beat phrase. The faster second thematic area continues the varied metrics, which now alternate in three-beat and two-beat patterns that combine to create ten-beat phrases. It has been suggested that this remarkable rhythmic structure hints at Brahms's familiarity with authentic Hungarian folk music, in which asymmetric patterns are common

The Allegro molto finale develops the original motto and a related idea with varied rhythms and figuration. The mode changes to C major at the coda, bringing the work to an affirmative conclusion.

WORKS WITH VARIED SCORING

Trio in E flat Major for Horn, Cello, and Piano, Opus 40

Andante
Scherzo: Allegro
Adagio mesto
Finale: Allegro con brio

Brahms studied horn as a boy in Hamburg, and he retained a fondness for the instrument throughout his life. He began to compose his Horn Trio soon after the death of his mother in 1865, possibly as a nostalgic remembrance of his childhood. Brahms specified that the horn part should be played on the seventeenth-century designed Waldhorn, an instrument he preferred to the more fluent valved horn because of its clear, majestic tone. The noble simplicity of his Horn Trio results from the restrained lines written for this cumbersome, yet hauntingly beautiful instrument. However, today's performers almost invariably perform on the modern French horn.

In the rhapsodic Andante two contrasting themes alternate to create a symmetrical five-part form reminiscent of the older divertimento style. Brahms wrote that the first theme occurred to him as he stood on "wooded heights amid fir trees" during a visit to the Black Forest. The movement concludes with plaintive calls in the horn.

The Scherzo begins with a spirited melody that suggests ancient hunting calls. A contrasting trio section (A flat minor) evokes the elegiac mood of the Andante. The energetic opening material returns.

Both the solemn Adagio mesto (E flat minor) and the rapid Allegro con brio are linked by a song from Brahms's childhood,

In den Weiden steht ein Haus ("In the Meadow Stands a House"). Heard near the end of the introspective third movement, this venerable German song is transformed by changes of tempo and articulation into the joyful main theme of the exultant finale.

Trio in A Minor for Clarinet, Cello, and Piano, Opus 114

Allegro
Adagio
Andantino grazioso
Allegro

In the summer of 1890 Brahms startled friends and publishers alike by announcing his decision to retire from composition. He promised to complete works that had been started but, according to his friend Theodor Billroth, "rejected the idea that he would ever compose anything again." Fortunately, Brahms soon regained his inspiration after hearing performances by clarinetist Richard Mühlfeld, a self-taught musician who at age 23 was acclaimed the greatest wind player of his time. Brahms, formerly unaware of the lyric potential of the clarinet, decided to create chamber works to showcase Mühlfeld's artistry. Because of declining health, these were to be his final instrumental compositions.

Brahms composed his Opus 114 Trio during his summer retreat to Bad Ischl in 1891. His selection of the clarinet in A rather than the more brilliant instrument in B flat allows the player to execute a darker, more veiled tone quality that blends effectively with the cello sonority in the trio's interlocking lines. Reflecting the influence of Beethoven's late quartets, Opus 114 develops an intense dialogue among the three instruments. In the first and second movements Brahms incorporated material that he had planned to develop in a projected fifth symphony. Perhaps because of this intention, the energetic opening Allegro and the serene Adagio are somewhat symphonic in scope. The graceful third movement

is a waltzlike intermezzo; the more rustic trio section, with suggestions of clarinet yodeling, resembles the Ländler, an Austrian folk
dance. The rondo finale, which also evokes folk style, is based on
two themes Hungarian in spirit.

Piano Quartet in G Minor, Opus 25

Allegro
Intermezzo: Allegro, ma non troppo—Trio: Animato
Andante con moto
Rondo alla Zingarese: Presto

Throughout his career, Brahms preferred to compose similarly
scored works in pairs, thereby creating compositional "twins" that
were generally complementary to one another in terms of character. When he was 24 years old he began to work simultaneously
on his G Minor and A Major Piano Quartets and, after numerous
revisions, completed them both four years later in the fall of 1861.
At that time preparing for his Viennese debut as both composer
and pianist, Brahms decided to premiere the bolder, more extroverted G Minor Quartet at this important event. On this occasion
the Opus 25 Quartet achieved resounding success. "Truly this is
Beethoven's heir!" exclaimed one musician present. Later, however, that particular musician confessed to having drunk too much
Croatian wine and moderated his praise.

Several of Brahms's musician intimates leveled criticism at
Opus 25: "Too overworked" (Joachim), "I was not transported"
(Clara Schumann). The strongest praise for Opus 25, a product of
Brahms's reverence for Beethoven and Schubert, ironically came
years later from Arnold Schoenberg. As homage, Schoenberg cre-
ated a full orchestral setting for Opus 25. Schoenberg explained:
"Opus 25 is seldom played, but badly so when it is. The better the
pianist the louder he plays and you hear nothing from the strings.
I wanted once to hear everything, and this I achieved." (Brahms

himself published Opus 25 as a piano duet but requested not to be identified as the arranger.)

The expansive Allegro, in sonata form, demonstrates that Brahms, like Beethoven, could develop small motivic units with unlimited imagination. The movement's dramatically contrasting melodic groups are derived entirely from two brief thematic cells.

Brahms originally titled his ethereal second movement Scherzo but changed its designation to Intermezzo because he perceived its character to be more delicate than Beethoven's robust scherzo movements. A gently veiled tone color is achieved through muting of the violin. The Andante movement explores two themes, one majestic and bold, the second more animated. The exciting finale, an alluring rondo "in gypsy style," is for many listeners the high point of Opus 25 (if not a favorite movement in all nineteenth-century chamber music). Reminiscent of Brahms's earlier Hungarian Dances, the movement offers four melodious themes. After a virtuoso piano cadenza, the movement ends "molto presto."

Piano Quartet in A Major, Opus 26

Allegro non troppo
Poco Adagio
Scherzo: Poco Allegro
Finale: Allegro

Perhaps Brahms's favorite piano quartet, the Opus 26 (1861) has been described as "Wagnerian" because it unfolds with similar romantic passion. It differs from its complementary G minor companion of the same date (Opus 25) primarily because of its subtler structure—one hears continuous evolution of themes rather than distinct and extroverted statements. The two piano quartets were premiered in Vienna within days of each other, and Brahms performed as pianist for both. Following the audience's warm reception of the A Major Quartet, he wrote: "I had much joy yesterday. The quartet was well reviewed, and I had extraordinary success as a pianist."

The two themes of the opening movement are energized by rhythmic interplay as pairs of notes are set against groups of three. The central section features Brahms's technique of "developing variation," by which the themes are transformed melodically and harmonically. A coda with close canonic treatment of themes concludes the movement.

Ever a perfectionist, Brahms had considered abbreviating the rapturous Poco Adagio movement long after its publication, but he was deterred by his friends. A free rondo, the piano's songful nocturne is embellished by the muted strings. Recurring and mysterious piano arpeggio figures are answered by the strings with growing intensity.

The opening section of the scherzo movement, Poco Allegro, is based on two themes; the contrasting trio features canonic writing. Propelled by energetic rhythms, the exhilarating finale develops two themes Viennese in spirit.

Piano Quartet in C Minor, Opus 60

Allegro non troppo
Scherzo: Allegro
Andante
Finale: Allegro comodo

During the two years of Robert Schumann's hospitalization for mental illness, Brahms supported the ailing composer's wife Clara and their children both financially and emotionally. Brahms developed a deep affection for Clara, but he remained solely a platonic friend out of loyalty to Schumann. His Opus 60 Quartet, written in its first version during this difficult period (1855–56), has acquired the subtitle "Werther" because Brahms felt conflicts similar to Goethe's distraught hero, who killed himself over unrequited love for his friend's wife. Brahms's angst did not diminish over time. When Brahms finally submitted the manuscript to his publisher twenty years later, he wrote: "You can put on the title page a picture, namely that of a man with a pistol to his head. Now you can get an idea of the music." Clara evidently did not realize the extent of the composer's anguish. "Johannes is such a riddle," she commented when perceiving his brooding demeanor. Although the quartet was substantially revised, it retains its powerful and introspective narrative.

In its original unpublished version, lost and most probably destroyed, the quartet was a three-movement work in C sharp minor. After several private performances Brahms expressed dissatisfaction with the work and filed it in a drawer. Revisiting the score twenty years later, he composed a new Scherzo and transposed the recast outer movement keys to C minor—a key that for Brahms (as for Beethoven) held forceful and dramatic connotations. At the time Brahms undertook the quartet's revisions, his Symphony No. 1 in C Minor was in progress. The first movements of both works are similar in their structural and harmonic details, evident especially at their openings and at their extensive codas, both of which end with surprising tranquillity.

The Allegro non troppo, a movement of solemn grandeur, develops two subjects in sonata form. The significant first idea is based on the notes that spell Robert Schumann's affectionate "Clara" theme—C-B-A-G sharp-A, here transposed a minor third to fit Brahms's C minor tonality. A broadly lyrical theme in the major mode follows. The passionate three-part Scherzo moves restlessly with displaced accents until the strings play a calm interlude in the contrasting major modality. Brahms especially admired the Andante (E major), which opens with a rhapsodic song for cello in its upper register. The Finale, turbulent and tinged with sadness, is propelled by contrapuntal passagework.

Piano Quintet in F Minor, Opus 34

Allegro non troppo
Andante, un poco Adagio
Scherzo: Allegro
Finale: Poco sostenuto—Allegro non troppo—
    Presto, non troppo

Although Brahms wrote his monumental Opus 34 Quintet early in his career, the work stands as one of his greatest achievements. Brahms had experimented relentlessly with its form and urged his musician friends to criticize his efforts frankly. In 1862 he showed his violinist friend Joachim the first version of Opus 34, scored for string quintet with two cellos. Joachim complained: "The work is too difficult, and without vigorous playing will not sound clear." Brahms promptly destroyed this version and rescored the work for two pianos. He then shared this version with his pianist friend Clara Schumann. She found new faults: "Its skillful combinations are interesting ... but it is a work whose ideas you must scatter, as from a horn of plenty, over an entire orchestra. Please take my advice and recast it." Although Brahms did retain this version (published as Opus 34b), he rescored the work for piano quintet, a combination that blends the string sonorities he desired with the dramatic impact of the piano. The final version of this epic work was published in 1865.

Because of Brahms's densely compact writing, the sonata form Allegro non troppo achieves massive impact within its moderate time frame. Influenced by Beethoven's processes of thematic development, the movement fully exploits its introductory motivic figures by combining and expanding them to heroic proportions over the course of the movement. At the outset two legato motifs, played in unison by the first violin, cello, and piano, are immediately varied by rapid figuration in the piano. The second subject (an expressive excursion into C sharp minor) reveals Brahms's fondness for simultaneous duple and triple rhythms; the equal note pairs of the lyrical theme are underpinned by relentless triplet patterns. At the beginning of the coda these motifs reappear quietly in a more sustained tempo and then accelerate to a brilliant conclusion.

The second movement (A flat major) opens with a serene song that recalls the lyric spirit of Schubert. Its poignant middle section, marked "expressive and accelerating," is followed by a return of the eloquent opening material, now subtly varied.

Propelled by an ominous pizzicato figure in the cello, the rugged Scherzo (C minor) develops a turbulent theme that is transformed first into a chorale and then a fugue. The broadly singing melody of the central trio (C major) relieves the drama.

The substantial finale is the most complex movement of the work. After a sustained, somewhat somber introduction, two vivacious folklike themes are developed in sonata rondo form with brilliant counterpoint and colorful key relationships. The work concludes with a powerful coda.

Quintet in B Minor for Clarinet and Strings, Opus 115

Allegro
Adagio
Andantino—Presto non assai, ma con sentimento
Con moto

Brahms's Opus 115 Quintet was the second of the four compositions resulting from his collaboration with the legendary clarinetist Richard Mühlfeld, the "dear nightingale" who inspired these final instrumental works. Although Brahms called it "a far greater folly" than his Opus 114 Trio, the Clarinet Quintet was an enormous success at its 1891 premiere, and the audience demanded that its substantial Adagio movement be repeated as an encore. A sketch made during this performance depicts Mühlfeld in the guise of a Greek god, homage to the beauty of both his performance and his person.

Often described as a love song to the clarinet, Opus 115 explores the instrument's vast nuance of tonal color through extended passages in each of its registers—the high clarino, the breathily mysterious middle range, and the dark, low chalumeau. Yet the wind lines are fully integrated with the strings to create a unified texture. The eloquent opening phrase of the poignantly autumnal opening movement consists of a simple violin melody answered by the clarinet to create a single idea—an illustration of the partnership between the wind and strings that continues throughout the work. The clarinet, however, holds the primary melodic interest in the two middle movements—a tranquil Adagio (B major) varied by a rhapsodic section suggesting Hungarian influence; and a graceful Andantino (D major) with an animated central section. The finale ("with motion") is a set of five ethereal variations on a theme woven from motifs exchanged between the first violin and clarinet. The haunting opening theme of the Allegro returns at the dramatic coda.

NINE

Czech Nationalism:
Smetana, Dvořák, Suk

Fueled by increased prosperity and the rise of an educated middle class, European nationalism grew into a powerful force during the mid-nineteenth century. Movements for self-governance were often aggressive, and the dominating nations in this age of empire generally responded with force. During the 1848 Prague Revolution, Bedřich Smetana campaigned against the Austrians ruling Bohemia, and that regime ostracized him for writing music that glorified his cause. After six years of exile in Sweden, Smetana returned to Bohemia after political tensions had diminished. Fired by fervent patriotism, he then began a movement to develop a national art. Smetana's younger contemporary, Antonín Dvořák, became a later participant; Dvořák's pupil Josef Suk continued the movement into the twentieth century. Because of deep roots in Austro-Hungary's musical traditions, these artists retained broadly European stylistic traits. However, they infused this inherited language with new harmonic and structural spontaneity, folk themes, and programmatic descriptions of Bohemian images or events.

BEDŘICH SMETANA
B. MARCH 2, 1824 IN LITOMYŠL, BOHEMIA,
D. MAY 12, 1884 IN PRAGUE

A brilliant piano interpreter of international figures such as Chopin and Liszt, Bedřich Smetana followed his uniquely nationalist voice as a composer. He aspired to achieve a distinctively Bohemian quality through patterns that mimic its abundant nature (as the flowing waters of the River Moldau) or that draw from its folk heritage (as heard in *The Bartered Bride*). In his two programmatic string quartets Smetana created a self-portrait set against a background of his native Bohemia.

String Quartet in E Minor ("From My Life"), JB 1:105

Allegro vivo appassionato
Allegro moderato a la Polka
Largo sostenuto
Vivace

After his sudden onset of deafness at age 50, Smetana projected two string quartets, each to be entitled *From My Life*. However, only the first quartet (1876) received that title. Intended to be heard as an autobiographical tonal portrait, the E Minor Quartet casts the violist as its protagonist—an honor Dvořák enjoyed at its premiere.

Smetana provided his quartet's program in a letter. The first movement, he writes, "depicts my youthful leanings toward art, the romantic atmosphere, the inexpressible yearnings ... and also a warning of my future misfortune (deafness)." The opening theme, an impassioned descending phrase in the viola, represents the misfortune that will soon overtake him. This poignant motive, which recurs throughout the quartet, is followed by a gentler second theme that suggests his delight in artistic pursuits. After development of the first theme and a recapitulation of the second, the movement concludes with somber pizzicato notes in the cello.

Smetana describes the second movement as "a quasi-polka that recalls the joyful days of youth when I composed dance tunes and was known everywhere as a passionate lover of dancing." The movement begins with a spirited dance motif. The viola introduces a vigorous contrasting idea that Smetana states should be played "like a trumpet." In the trio section the violins intone chord progressions over a rhythmic pattern articulated by the viola and cello. An abbreviated version of the opening section and a brief coda conclude the movement.

Smetana continues: "The third movement (the one which, in the opinion of the gentlemen who play this quartet, is unperformable) reminds me of the happiness of my first love, the girl who later became my wife." Essentially an extended love song, the movement develops two ardent and lyrical themes with rich romantic harmonies and challenging rhythmic figuration. A pensive coda suggests yearning for happier times that have passed.

"The fourth movement describes the discovery that I could develop nationalistic elements in music and my joy in following this path until it was checked by the catastrophe of the onset of my deafness and the prospect of my sad future; and remembering all the promise of my early career, a feeling of painful regret." The movement opens with a joyous dance that suggests native Bohemian folk music. Vigorous passages alternate with graceful sections, and the dance ends abruptly. After a moment of silence, the first violin plays a piercingly high E over an ominous tremolo in the other strings. "This is the fateful ringing in my ears that announced the beginning of my deafness. I permitted myself this little joke, such as it is, because it was so disastrous for me." After a synopsis of themes from the earlier movements, the work ends in a mood of quiet resignation.

String Quartet in D Minor, JB 1:124

Allegro
Allegro moderato
Allegro non più moderato, ma agitato e con fuoco
Finale: Presto

Smetana suffered from syphilis, which took an enormous toll on his health in his later years. He intended for the less frequently performed D Minor Quartet to be a programmatic continuation of the first, a depiction of "the turbulence of a person who has lost his hearing." Smetana's last important work, the quartet was written during the years 1882–1883, at which time his physical state was rapidly declining.

The opening Allegro is characterized by passionate aphoristic statements; the second movement develops more clearly in rondo form. Its main theme is a polka that Smetana had written decades earlier together with a songful new idea. After an animated introduction, the third movement dramatically depicts Smetana's mental state through agitated fugal passages. The final Presto, written against the advice of his physicians, abbreviates Smetana's original conception. This brief and energetic finale can be heard as a catharsis to an essentially troubled work.

ANTONÍN DVOŘÁK
B. SEPTEMBER 8, 1841 IN NELAHOZEVES, BOHEMIA,
D. MAY 1, 1904 IN PRAGUE

At age 32 Dvořák critically evaluated his body of work and concluded that much was an inferior derivative of Wagner and other German post-romantic composers. He then destroyed the majority of his unpublished compositions (carefully providing a list of those he had burned). Motivated by his compatriot Bedřich Smetana, who stressed the composer's responsibility to promote his own national idiom, Dvořák began to create works that reflected the spontaneity and directness of Bohemian music.

STRING QUARTETS

String Quartet in D Minor, Opus 34

Allegro
Alla polka: Allegretto scherzando
Adagio
Finale: Poco Allegro

Dvořák composed his Opus 34, the ninth of his fourteen string quartets, as a gesture of appreciation to his friend Johannes Brahms, who had helped to place the *Moravian Duets* with the publisher Simrock. After hearing the welcome news Dvořák began composition immediately, and Opus 34 was completed within two weeks in 1877. Dvořák dedicated the quartet to Brahms, who indicated that he was not completely satisfied with the work. "You write rather hurriedly," he said in a letter. "It would be advisable to look more closely at the notes for numerous missing sharps, flats, and naturals, and at the part writing, etc." Nevertheless, Brahms again helped to secure publication for Opus 34.

Dvořák at this time was at the threshold of his nationalistic phase, and Opus 34 reflects his new preoccupation in its inner movements. The opening Allegro suggests the influence of Schubert, whose A Minor Quartet begins with a similar undulating figure in the second violin and viola. The movement develops two related themes—a fragment from the first idea is expanded into a second subject. The two subjects intertwine in the B major development. The movement concludes with an emphatic coda.

The whimsical Polka leads into a rapid trio section that resembles a Slavonic dance. The haunting Adagio explores two closely related themes, first articulated by the violins, then by the viola with a soaring violin countermelody. The second subject from the opening Allegro returns at the coda. Propelled by energetic rhythms, the vigorous finale develops in sonata form.

String Quartet in E flat Major, Opus 51

Allegro ma non troppo
Dumka (Elegie): Andante con moto—Vivace
Romanza: Andante con moto
Finale: Allegro assai

After the publication of his Slavonic Dances (1878), Dvořák's fame spread rapidly throughout Europe. He received numerous commissions, among which was a request from the celebrated Florentine Quartet for a chamber work in the "Slavonic style." Dvořák began this quartet, the Opus 51, on Christmas Day, 1878 and completed it three months later. Brahms's influential violinist friend Joseph Joachim hosted the premiere for a glittering crowd at his Berlin home. The modest Dvořák was overwhelmed by its enthusiastic reception.

One of Dvořák's most vivid works, Opus 51 is remarkable for its joyous melodies, inventive counterpoint, and rich tonal coloring. Subtle rhythmic treatment animates the opening movement. Its two themes are juxtaposed in the development section—the primary theme is stated in long note values while the dancelike second theme accompanies as a bass line. The recapitulation begins with the second subject and the haunting coda is derived from the main theme.

The second movement is a *dumka*—a pensive movement with vivacious sections intruding to relieve the melancholy. An elegiac violin melody (G minor) over pizzicato chords in the cello alternates with a *furiant*, an energetic Bohemian dance. The Romanza (B flat major) explores a rhapsodic theme with subtle harmonies. The vivacious finale is written in sonata rondo form— its two themes are expanded and developed but earlier passages recur at intervals. The movement evokes the *skoky*, a Bohemian jumping dance.

String Quartet in F Major, Opus 96 ("American")

Allegro ma non troppo
Lento
Molto vivace
Finale: Vivace ma non troppo

Both to celebrate the fourth centenary of Columbus by integrating old and new world music and also to encourage a specifically American musical voice, Dvořák came to the United States in 1892 to serve as Director of the National Conservatory of Music, newly formed under the auspices of philanthropist Jeannette Thurber. During his three-year sojourn, Dvořák immersed himself in American regional tunes, and he developed special admiration for spirituals, plantation songs, and native Indian chants. "American music should draw from these wellsprings," he insisted. He himself incorporated these elements into his own compositions written at this time—especially the Symphony *From the New World* (1893) and the "American" String Quartet, written the same year during his summer vacation in the small Bohemian community of Spillville, Iowa. Dvořák stated that he never quoted actual motifs in either work. He wrote: "I have simply written original themes embodying the peculiarities of native music, and, using these themes as subjects, have developed them with all the resources of modern rhythm, harmony, counterpoint, and color."

Dvořák worked well in his rented stone house set among corn and potato fields. Content in the large, supportive company of family and servants, he drafted his quartet in four days and completed it within two weeks. He performed in the work's informal Spillville premiere as violist with an amateur quartet.

The Allegro ma non troppo offers homage to his compatriot Smetana's quartet *From My Life*, which opens similarly with a pedal note in the cello and undulating violin figuration supporting a robust viola melody. Yet Dvořák wrote that the movement "breathes an Indian spirit." Its three themes are each based on a five-note pentatonic scale, a common feature of indigenous song.

The ethereal theme of the Lento (D minor) echoes both the melancholy of the plantation spiritual and the pentatonic tonal structure of Plains Indian song. Syncopated figures in the second violin and viola underpin statements of this haunting theme, heard first in the violin then the cello.

Dvořák wrote that he was impressed by the energetic song of a scarlet tanager that nested in the woods near Spillville. He carefully notated this birdcall and used it as the basis for the Molto vivace. This scherzo movement develops through the repetition of two alternating tunes (A-B-A-B-A), although the B section is actually a slower version of the A melody.

A small tribe of Sioux Indians residing near Spillville as part of a travelling show frequently performed for Dvořák. Possibly they inspired the vivacious rondo finale, which begins with a rhythmic pattern suggesting Indian drumming. At the movement's center the tempo slows, and a chorale tune is introduced. A restatement of earlier themes and a lively coda conclude the work.

String Quartet in G Major, Opus 106

Allegro moderato
Adagio ma non troppo
Molto vivace
Finale: Andante sostenuto—Allegro con fuoco

Soon after Dvořák had returned to Prague from his Directorship of the National Conservatory in New York City he wrote:
"We are all inexpressibly happy to be home! Now I am very indus-
trious. I work so easily I never could ask for anything better. I have
just completed a new quartet in G major and have already begun
another." Dvořák wrote the Opus 106 quartet, the thirteenth of
his fourteen string quartets, within a three-week period. It was
premiered in Prague the following year by the Bohemian Quartet.

Although Opus 106 occasionally suggests American influence in its inner movements, Slavic folk song and dance provide
its primary materials. Modal shifts from major to minor occur
throughout the work, imparting a haunting atmosphere of light
and shade. The Allegro moderato richly develops two themes, one
joyous and the second songful but more restrained. In the Adagio
ma non troppo, essentially a set of free variations on a theme in E
flat major, Dvořák molds alternately major and minor aspects of
the subject into a dynamic and deeply moving statement.

The Molto vivace (B minor) presents three recurrences of a
vigorous scherzo section alternating with two trios—first, a lyrical
duet between the first violin and viola, then a section that resembles folk song. The Finale is a rondo that develops a pair of themes
in G major and G minor alternating with a contrasting subject in
E flat major. At its center Dvořák reintroduces themes from the
first movement and incorporates them into the work's vigorous
conclusion.

String Quartet in A flat Major, Opus 105

Adagio ma non troppo—Allegro appassionato
Molto vivace
Lento e molto cantabile
Allegro non tanto

In early 1895 Dvořák had completed his three-year directorship of the National Conservatory in New York City and was eager to return to Prague. Although he had composed productively during his American sojourn, Dvořák never overcame intense homesickness for his native Bohemia. Shortly before his departure he began his Opus 105 quartet, which was intended as a statement of his Bohemian nationalism. Because of various distractions he was able to complete only 70 measures, and once back in Prague other matters consumed his time. He wrote to a friend: "My muse is now quite silent. For four whole months I have not even taken up my pen." When he did resume composing, he chose to make a fresh start on another quartet, Opus 106. Only when that opus was completed did he return to Opus 105, which he finished within three weeks. It was to be the last of his fourteen quartets. Dvořák requested that the premiere of Opus 105 be given by his own Prague Conservatory students on the anniversary of his return to Bohemia, April 16, 1896.

Although infrequently programmed, the Opus 105 Quartet is considered to be one of Dvořák's finest compositions. Hauntingly beautiful Slavic folk songs and dance themes pervade the work's essentially classical structure. After a somber introduction led by the solo cello (A flat minor) and a subtle modulation to the major key, the opening movement develops two closely related themes in sonata form. The superb F minor scherzo movement, Molto vivace, is based on the energetic *furiant*, a Bohemian dance in which duple rhythmic patterns intrude into the established triple meter. The F major slow movement (marked "very singing") is thematically related to the opening movement. Homage to his friend Brahms, the Lento develops warm and broad themes that are varied by subtle changes of scoring. After an introductory statement in the solo cello, the extensive rondo finale explores an array of exuberant motifs.

WORKS WITH VARIED SCORING

String Quintet in E flat Major, Opus 97

Allegro non tanto
Allegro vivo—Un poco meno mosso
Larghetto
Finale: Allegro giusto

Written during Dvořák's summer visit to Spillville, Iowa, the Opus 97 String Quintet (scored for string quartet and additional viola, 1893) incorporates American regional themes while fully retaining its Bohemian identity. Dvořák was especially fascinated by the rhythmic drumming of native Indians. On three occasions he arranged for the Sioux members of a touring "Medicine Man" show to perform their songs and dances for him at a local inn. Suggestions of these themes abound in the first two movements of Opus 97. Although the opening motif of the Allegro non tanto resembles Bohemian melodies heard in Dvořák's earlier works, the second idea, built on a long-short dotted rhythm, is based on an actual Indian tune. After a slow introduction that foreshadows the vigorous main theme, the sonata form opening movement develops two ideas, both energized by hints of a drumbeat in the first viola line. At the conclusion the introductory material returns as a reprise. The Allegro vivo (B major) is a three-part scherzo (A-B-A) launched by a solo drumming theme in the second viola; the first viola plays the pensive theme of the central section. Colorful harmonies vary the return of the opening material.

The Larghetto is an eloquent set of variations on a hymnlike theme that Dvořák had conceived as an alternate setting for the American patriotic song *My Country 'Tis of Thee*. Throughout the variations Dvořák exploits the rich textural possibilities of the viola quintet ensemble to complement the various transformations of the theme. The Finale is a spirited rondo with a principal theme based on the dotted rhythm heard in the opening movement.

String Sextet in A Major, Opus 48

Allegro moderato
Dumka (Elegie): Poco Allegretto
Furiant: Presto
Finale: Tema con variazioni

Dvořák composed his only string sextet in 1878, the same year he wrote his enormously popular *Slavonic Dances* and *Slavonic Rhapsodies*. This was a period of growing nationalism for Dvořák, and his compositions of this time reveal new folk spirit. Written within two weeks, the A Major Sextet was Dvořák's first chamber work to receive its premiere outside of his native Bohemia. Enthusiastically received by Berlin's musical elite, the new work was performed in London the following year led by Joachim, Europe's most famous violinist. Its success there contributed to Dvořák's rapidly increasing fame.

The richly textured Allegro moderato develops two themes in sonata form. Dvořák's emerging nationalism is heard primarily in the Sextet's two inner movements. The *Dumka*, remarkable for its five-bar phrase structures and innovative harmonies, is a Slavic folk song with pervading melancholy relieved by interludes contrasting in mood and tempo. The *Furiant* is a rapid Slavonic dance with alternating duple and triple meters; its D major trio provides a calming contrast.

In a return to classical structure, Dvořák modelled his "Theme with variations" finale on the final movement of Beethoven's Opus 74 Quartet ("The Harp"). Dvořák's graceful theme, initially presented by the first viola, undergoes five variations. The movement concludes with a brilliant Presto.

Piano Trio in E Minor, Opus 90 ("Dumky")

Lento maestoso—Allegro
Poco Adagio—Vivace non troppo
Andante—Vivace non troppo
Andante moderato—Allegretto scherzando—Allegro
Allegro
Lento maestoso—Vivace

Dvořák wrote his Opus 90 Piano Trio (*Dumky*, 1891) during his most intensely nationalistic phase, at which time he aspired to infuse his works with the vitality inherent in Slavonic rhythms and melodies. Dvořák himself was unsure about the precise meaning of the word *dumka* (plural *dumky*), since he was confronted by differing usages in the Slavonic folk repertoire. In all Slavonic languages the word *dumka* is derived from root verbs meaning "to meditate, ponder, or brood." In the Ukrainian language a *dumka* is a recollection of heroic deeds either narrated or sung in verse. In the Serbian context it suggests dark moodiness conveyed through dramatic changes of tempo. However, Dvořák also admired a cheerful Polish *dumka* that was not unlike a polka. After Dvořák had composed several *dumky*, he took a folk specialist to a coffeeshop and asked him directly, "What, exactly, is a *dumka*?"

For Dvořák the form gradually evolved into a genre that was basically pensive or melancholy but included lively and joyous sections. His Opus 90 Trio consists of six *dumky* that are connected primarily by similar progressions of mood. The first three succeed each other without interruption. A declamatory cello phrase, followed by a somber duet with the violin, introduces the first *dumka*, and a rapid second section provides exuberant contrast. The second *dumka* begins with a plaintive cello recitative, a lament that alternates with sections of wild gaiety. The third *dumka* opens in a reflective mood but vivace sections enliven the atmosphere. The final three *dumky* resemble the andante, scherzo, and finale movements of a traditional piano trio. Yet each can also be heard as an individual and passionate Slavonic rhapsody of chamber music literature.

Piano Quartet in E flat Major, Opus 87

Allegro con fuoco
Lento
Allegro moderato, grazioso
Finale: Allegro ma non troppo

Encouraged by his eager publishers, Dvořák composed the majority of Opus 87, the second of his two piano quartets, within the period of a month. He wrote to a friend: "I've now already finished three movements of a new piano quartet and the finale will be ready in a few days. As I expected, it came easily, and the melodies just surged upon me, thank God!" The work was completed in 1889 and the premiere was held the following fall.

Dvořák's Opus 87 can be heard as complementary to his other great piano chamber works of the late 1880s such as the *Dumky* Trio and the A Major Piano Quintet. There is textural similarity in all these compositions since the strings form a unit to balance the strong piano lines. These spirited works are products of his nationalistic phase, a time when he found inspiration in his native Bohemian folk idiom.

The strings introduce the bold principal motive of the Allegro con fuoco and the piano offers an even more forceful reply. The viola (Dvořák's instrument) brings in the second subject, a flowing idea in G major. Highly colorful changes of harmony occur in the development. After a brief recapitulation, the movement concludes with a coda that begins "tranquillo" but rapidly crescendos to an emphatic statement.

The remarkable Lento (G flat major) explores five distinct ideas. A dialogue between the cello and piano leads to a calm theme for violin, followed by an agitated piano statement. A passionate motif for the entire ensemble decrescendos into the plaintive fifth theme, heard in the piano. The movement concludes in hushed tones.

The delightful scherzo movement plays with two themes suggesting Czech folk dance; its lively trio section unfolds as a canon. The powerful Finale, in sonata form, begins in the unusual key of E flat minor. Its two subjects are ingeniously varied, occasionally with notable passagework for viola. The work's original key of E flat major returns at the recapitulation, and the movement concludes with an energetic coda.

Piano Quintet in A Major, Opus 81

Allegro, ma non tanto
Dumka: Andante con moto—Vivace
Scherzo (Furiant): Molto vivace
Finale: Allegro

Dvořák's Opus 81 Piano Quintet ranks as one of the finest creations in the quintet repertoire. Completed in 1887, the work had incubated for sixteen years; an early three-movement version had been premiered and included in his personal catalogue as Opus 5 but not published. As his reputation grew and the demand for his chamber music increased, Dvořák decided to revisit his rejected earlier works. The publisher Simrock welcomed all revisions, but the self-critical Dvořák still hesitated to submit the quintet. After much prodding he finally produced a drastically revised four-movement quintet that benefited from his current nationalistic impulse, which had resulted in the spirited *Dumky* Trio and the *Slavonic Dances*.

Dvořák's close friends described the Quintet as a virtual portrait of its composer. A man who experienced continuously changing nuances of mood, Dvořák created a work that also moves through a wide emotional spectrum—pensive brooding quickly changes to fierce exuberance, which momentarily fades to serenity. Dvořák, who was most at home in the countryside, wrote Opus 81 at his new summer home at the edge of the forest in Vysoka. The peaceful beauty of his rural surroundings perhaps is reflected in the Quintet's glowing sonorities.

The Allegro opens with a poignant cello statement that hovers between the tonalities of A major and A minor. After several episodes, the viola offers a second theme in C sharp minor. These two warmly lyrical themes are continuously recast within a wide range of harmonic colorings and tempos.

The second movement (F sharp minor) is a Slavic *dumka*, traditionally a rhapsodic form with an elegiac atmosphere; lively, even jubilant passages intervene to relieve the melancholy. In the Opus 81 *Dumka*, the pensive opening idea alternates with abruptly rapid sections to create a rondo structure.

Dvořák termed the following Scherzo a *furiant*, perhaps his favorite Bohemian dance. This vigorous form characteristically moves with alternating duple and triple rhythms, although in Opus 81 a triple meter prevails. A softer central section marked "somewhat tranquil" (F major) slows the momentum.

The exuberant finale develops with animated rhythms and vivid Slavonic melodies. A fugal passage at its center and a subdued chorale at the coda enhance the dimension of this brilliant movement.

JOSEF SUK
B. JANUARY 4, 1874 IN KŘEČOVICE, BOHEMIA,
D. MAY 29, 1935 IN BENEŠOV, CZECHOSLOVAKIA

The favorite pupil of Antonín Dvořák and eventually his son-in-law, Josef Suk is honored as one of the most significant Czech post-romantic composers. By the age of 22 he had attracted the attention of the influential Johannes Brahms, who recommended publication of Suk's recent works with the venerable Simrock firm. After his appointment as Director of Advanced Composition at the Prague Conservatory, Suk mentored students such as Bohuslav Martinů and Rudolf Firkušný. Suk was also a virtuoso violinist, and he continued to perform numerous concerts with the Czech Quartet, which he had helped to found while still a student. Inevitably, composition for Suk became a part-time activity. He did create a small body of primarily instrumental compositions that reveal a steady development from late Romanticism toward a complex and personal musical language.

Piano Trio in C Minor, Opus 2

Allegro
Andante
Vivace

Suk wrote his Opus 2 Piano Trio while he was a student at the Prague Conservatory. He substantially revised it twice during 1890–91 with the guidance of Antonín Dvořák, who recommended that Suk delete the most obvious references to his own work. The influence of Beethoven is perhaps heard in the trio's heroic opening theme (C minor). The Allegro develops in classical sonata form with warm harmonies that occasionally suggest Dvořák, especially in its second theme group (introduced by the cello). The Andante is a clearly-structured romantic song that builds to a robust piano statement near its conclusion. The energetic Vivace, written in sonata form, opens with a piquant syncopated theme in the unison violin and cello.

String Quartet in B flat Major, Opus 11

Allegro moderato
Intermezzo: Tempo di Marcia
Adagio, ma non troppo
Allegro giocoso

Suk's Opus 11 String Quartet (1896) reveals the strong influence of Antonín Dvořák in its warmly harmonized, melodious lines and exuberant Slavic spirit. Despite its early publication and popular acceptance, Suk revisited the quartet in 1915 and substantially revised large portions in a modernist style; however, today's performers most often prefer Suk's original version. His quartet follows the classical quartet scheme of lively outer movements and two inner movements that contrast in tempo and atmosphere.

The Allegro moderato develops two Slavic folk-tinged themes in sonata form. Fluent passagework animates the Intermezzo, which Suk later chose to publish separately as a Barcarolle for string quartet. The introspective Adagio ma non troppo develops with lyrical lines and rich harmonies that suggest the influence of Dvořák. The finale is a brisk and witty statement that moves with Bohemian dance rhythms.

TEN

Romantic Russians: Borodin, Tchaikovsky, Arensky, Rachmaninov

Music of the Russian Romanticists is renowned for the vitality of its melodies, largely drawn from a vast trove of folk song, and its hauntingly expressive harmonies, richly colored by Russia's Byzantine liturgy. Russia's national school of composition cohered slowly during the Romantic era. Until nearly the middle of the nineteenth century Russia's art music was almost exclusively imported from the European continent, and Italian music dominated concert life. No true Russian style existed until Mikhail Glinka produced his folk-based operas, the most famous of which is *Russlan and Ludmilla* (1836). A more rugged nationalism emerged in 1860 with "The Mighty Five" (Mily Balakirev, Alexander Borodin, César Cui, Modest Mussorgsky, and Nikolai Rimsky-Korsakov), essentially self-taught composers who looked beyond European Russia toward its expansive Asian territories and the eastern Caucasus for inspiration. The exoticism heard in the works of Balakirev in particular was admired and emulated by the cosmopolitan Tchaikovsky as well as his younger conservatory colleagues Arensky and Rachmaninov. Although essentially tied to mainstream European techniques, these latter three composers blended their works with the distinctive colors and essences of Russia's far-ranging folk tradition.

ALEXANDER BORODIN
B. NOVEMBER 12, 1833 IN ST. PETERSBURG,
D. FEBRUARY 27, 1887 IN ST. PETERSBURG

String Quartet No. 2 in D Major

Allegro moderato
Scherzo: Allegro
Notturno: Andante
Finale: Andante—Vivace

Alexander Borodin belongs to the "Mighty Five," that small but
formidable group of nationalist Russian composers who banded
together during the late midpoint of the nineteenth century. A
powerful force in the development of Russian culture, the group's
goal was to create a specifically Slavic musical language based on
folk songs, dances, and legends. Borodin differed from its other
members (Balakirev, Cui, Mussorgsky, and Rimsky-Korsakov)
because of his greater receptivity to Western European styles and
forms; he reported that he "horrified Mussorgsky with the news
that he was composing a string quartet." Unlike his fellow composers Borodin created his own melodies, all imbued with the
atmosphere of Russian folk song. Because of his full employment as
a research chemist, Borodin produced only a small but fine body of
compositions. Yet his bold writing, strong lyricism, and exotic coloring (especially heard in the *Polovtsian Dances*) contributed to his
reputation as one of Russia's great nineteenth-century innovators.

Borodin's D Major Quartet (1881) is one of his finest achievements. Perhaps influenced by the classical clarity of Mendelssohn,
whom he admired, the first, second, and fourth movements
develop in sonata form. However, the work emerges as strongly
Russian because of its sustained, modally-inflected lyricism and
the insistent motivic repetitions characteristic of Slavic folk song.

Borodin was an accomplished cellist, and his second quartet

offers luxuriant solos for the instrument. The cello sings the opening theme of the Allegro moderato, and the violin introduces the minor-key second theme over a pizzicato accompaniment. After the two themes are developed and recapitulated, the movement ends with a brief coda. Borodin stated that the winsome Scherzo "attempts to conjure the impression of a lighthearted evening in a pleasure garden of St. Petersburg." Its two motifs—one rapid and ethereal, the second waltzlike—are developed with colorful harmonies.

One of the best-known movements in the string quartet literature, the serene Notturno opens with a sublime cello song that achieved fame in mid-twentieth century popular music as "This Is My Beloved" from the musical *Kismet*. The movement unfolds in three-part song form. In the Finale the two themes of the Vivace section are treated fugally, and the movement concludes with a brilliant coda.

PYOTR ILYICH TCHAIKOVSKY
B. MAY 7, 1840 IN VOTINSK,
D. NOVEMBER 6, 1893 IN ST. PETERSBURG

Tchaikovsky often stated that he preferred music written for large forces of instruments to the intimate medium of chamber music. Nevertheless, he was one of the first Russian composers to write chamber works, and together with Alexander Borodin he is considered to be the true originator of the Russian school of chamber music. Tchaikovsky's contributions to the genre are few but important—three string quartets, a single piano trio, and the string sextet *Souvenir de Florence*. The string quartets, written at the beginning of his artistic maturity, all incorporate nationalistic Russian folk melodies and rhythms within a classically structured style.

String Quartet No. 1 in D Major, Opus 11

Moderato e simplice
Andante cantabile
Scherzo: Allegro non tanto e con fuoco
Finale: Allegro giusto

Tchaikovsky wrote his String Quartet No. 1 in 1871, a year of little income despite a professorship at the Moscow Conservatory and additional private students. To raise funds without the expense of hiring an orchestra he presented a public concert of his solo pieces. He offered this string quartet as his major chamber work. The new quartet quickly achieved wide popularity, especially because of its memorably tuneful Andante cantabile—a movement that has been transcribed for numerous combinations of instruments.

The sustained syncopations and undulating dynamics at the opening of the first movement have given Opus 11 its subtitle "Accordion." The movement's three themes are richly harmonized and fully developed in sonata form. After a brief recapitulation the movement concludes with a rapid coda.

Tchaikovsky based the melody for the Andante cantabile on the Russian folk song *Sidel Vanya*, which begins with the words "Vanya sat on a divan and smoked a pipe of tobacco." Between statements of the song the violin plays a second expressive theme over a pizzicato accompaniment.

The Scherzo resembles a robust peasant dance. In the central trio section the three upper instruments play intricate figurations over a sustained line in the cello. The Finale develops two vivacious themes and concludes with a vibrant coda.

Piano Trio in A Minor, Opus 50

Pezzo elegiaco: Moderato assai
Tema con variazioni
Variazione finale e coda

Tchaikovsky's patron, Nadezhda von Meck, persistently requested that he write a piano trio, but the composer replied that he found the form uncongenial. Since they communicated exclusively through letters, his views are well recorded: "It is a torture for me to have to listen to a trio or sonata of any kind for piano and strings. How unnatural is the union of such individualities as the piano, violin, and cello!"

Circumstances changed for Tchaikovsky as he sank into inertia following the death of his close friend and mentor, the pianist Nikolai Rubinstein, in 1881. Tchaikovsky now wrote to Madame von Meck that he no longer wished to write symphonic works since he had lost his most perceptive advocate. He resolved to create a trio centered on a massive piano part as a tribute to his departed friend. The resulting Piano Trio in A Minor was sketched within three weeks and given its premiere on the first anniversary of Rubenstein's death. Dedicated "to the memory of a great artist," the Trio gained immediate popularity and has consistently been recognized as Tchaikovsky's greatest chamber work. Since it was performed at the memorial concerts held following his death in 1893, the work ultimately became an elegy for Tchaikovsky himself.

The first movement, the grandly scaled *Pezzo elegiaco* (Elegiac piece) is structured in sonata form with tempo variations that dramatically delineate its various sections. Its substantial virtuoso piano part contributes to the movement's enormous sense of scale. Three distinctive, hauntingly melancholy themes are developed: the first idea, marked "rather moderate," leads to a fervent allegro theme as the second motif. A development section focuses on the opening idea but in the new faster tempo; a poetic third theme is introduced near the end of this section. The recapitulation, marked "slow and with sadness," unfolds with eloquent dialogues among the three instruments.

The second movement is divided into two parts—a "theme with variations" section (E major) and "a final variation and coda" (A major) amply structured in sonata form. The basic theme is possibly derived from a peasant's song that Tchaikovsky heard while he and Rubinstein enjoyed a country picnic; but its sophisticated organization as a set of ten two-bar phrases suggests original design. This melody undergoes eleven variations, the first three of which maintain the essential form of the theme. By the fourth variation different elements are isolated and developed into character statements. Among the most notable are Variation V, a high-pitched musette; and Variation VI, an extended waltz based on a motif from his opera *Eugene Onegin*. Variation VIII is an imposing three-part fugue anchored by piano octaves, and Variation X is a darkly hued mazurka.

The conclusion of the trio, "Final Variation and Coda," begins with a large-proportioned twelfth variation on the primary theme. After a powerful return of the first movement's opening material, the theme is restated as a poignant funeral march in the extensive coda.

ANTON ARENSKY
B. JULY 12, 1861 IN NOVGOROD, RUSSIA,
D. FEBRUARY 23, 1906 IN TERIOKI, FINLAND

Born into a musical family, Russian composer, pianist, and conductor Anton Arensky studied composition with the brilliant tonal colorist Rimsky-Korsakov at the St. Petersburg Conservatory. After graduation, he was appointed Professor of Composition at the Moscow Conservatory, where his notable pupils included Rachmaninov, Scriabin, and Glière. His colleague Tchaikovsky became his friend and mentor. After an important but brief period as Director of the Imperial Chapel, Arensky retired at age 40 with a generous pension and planned to devote his life to concertizing and composition. Unfortunately, his alcoholism led to a fatal case of tuberculosis, and he died at age 45. Appalled at the waste of tremendous gifts, Rimsky-Korsakov predicted that Arensky would soon be forgotten; but his reputation as an important Russian late Romantic has remained secure. Arensky is now remembered for a small number of works, several of which are miniatures, and his significant pedagogical influence.

One of imperial Russia's more eclectic composers, Arensky was most strongly influenced by Europe's leading romantic composers, particularly Chopin and Mendelssohn. Arensky's works all reveal fluent technique, singing melodic lines, and an affinity for unusual rhythmic patterns. A keen sense of instrumental color pervades his work.

Piano Trio No. 1 in D Minor, Opus 32

Allegro moderato
Scherzo: Allegro molto
Elegia: Adagio
Finale: Allegro non troppo

Arensky wrote his D Minor Trio, Opus 32 (1894) in memory of his cellist friend Karl Davidov, whom Tchaikovsky called "The Czar of Cellists." Davidov, who had died five years earlier, established the expressively intense Russian school of cello playing, and Arensky pays him tribute in the numerous songful passages for cello. Davidov's legendary performances were enhanced by his Golden Age Stradivarius, willed to him by Count Mathieu Wielhorsky, who procured the instrument through the exchange of his Guarneri cello, 40,000 francs, and the handsomest horse in his stables.

A soulful cello solo introduces the opening Allegro moderato, a substantial sonata form movement that inventively develops three lyrical themes. The movement concludes with a reflective coda (Adagio) that reprises the cello's opening idea.

The Scherzo's piquant opening theme, stated by the strings, is enlivened by spiccato bowing (light bounces off the strings). Piano runs offer a glittering accompaniment. Arensky was fond of dance, and the trio section features a leisurely waltz.

The Elegia (G minor) begins with a somber muted statement in the cello against quiet detached chords in the piano; a reflective dialogue between the violin and cello follows. A piano interlude in the major-key central section evokes peaceful memories.

Two contrasting ideas are developed in the dramatic rondo finale. Motives from both the first movement's opening statement and the Elegia return as a reprise.

String Quartet in A Minor for Violin, Viola, and Two Cellos, Opus 35

Moderato
Variations on a theme of Pyotr Tchaikovsky
Finale: Andante sostenuto—Allegro moderato

Soon after the death of Tchaikovsky, Arensky began his A Minor Quartet (1894). The work was intended as a memorial to his friend, and the use of the second cello in place of the customary second violin contributes strongly to the quartet's elegiac quality. Later he rescored the work for the standard quartet instrumentation and also for string orchestra. In its orchestral format the work has become his best-known composition.

The first movement opens with a muted psalm theme borrowed from ancient Russian church music. In its central section the mode shifts to A major, but the minor-key psalm theme returns to conclude the movement.

The second movement develops seven variations on a folklike children's song by Tchaikovsky, who had been steeped in native Russian melody from his earliest childhood. The song, *When Jesus Christ was Still a Child*, was taken from his Legend No. 5, *Sixteen Songs for Children*, Opus 54. A muted coda recalling the ancient Russian chant concludes the movement.

After an introductory Andante sostenuto section, the Finale fugally develops the Russian hymn *Slava Bogu no nebe Slava* ("Glory to God in Heaven"), which also appears in the Allegretto movement of Beethoven's second Rasumovsky quartet, Opus 59 No. 2.

SERGEI RACHMANINOV
B. APRIL 1, 1873 IN STARONRUSSKY UYEZD, RUSSIA,
D. MARCH 28, 1943 IN BEVERLY HILLS, CALIFORNIA

Piano Trio No. 2 in D Minor, Opus 9 ("Élégiaque")

Moderato
Quasi variazione: Andante
Allegro risoluto

While still a student at the Moscow Conservatory, Rachmaninov composed his first piano trio (also subtitled "élégiaque") in the style of Tchaikovsky, his adored friend and mentor. In late 1892 Tchaikovsky died suddenly during a cholera epidemic, most probably because he refused to take the precaution of drinking boiled water (leading to the rumor that he had committed suicide). That same day, November 6, the grief-stricken Rachmaninov began his Trio No. 2, Opus 9. A memorial to Tchaikovsky, the trio was completed in 1893 with the dedication "to the memory of a great artist." Rachmaninov himself performed the trio's massive piano part at its premiere, held in Moscow in January, 1894. He revised the work extensively from 1907–17.

Like his first piano trio, Rachmaninov's Opus 9 Piano Trio reveals affinities to his mentor's monumental Piano Trio in A Minor. Both are turbulent and melodious works constructed with fine craftsmanship and clear harmonic structure. Haunting, passionate and mystic, these trios can be heard as nationalistic Russian statements. Rachmaninov himself confided in a rare interview: "I am a Russian composer, and the land of my birth has influenced my temperament and outlook. My music is the product of my temperament, and so it is Russian music."

After a somber piano introduction, the strings intone the Moderato movement's opening themes—an elegiac idea followed by a sustained song. The movement develops with dramatic tempo changes that expressively delineate its large structure. Rapid string figuration and cascading piano lines alternate with calmer moments. A declamatory solo cello line suggests inward grief; but turbulent passagework soon follows to conjure rage. In the final section the opening theme returns in the piano and the strings articulate a muted accompaniment. The movement ends in a mood of quiet resignation.

The second movement (F major) offers eight variations on a theme introduced in a substantial passage for solo piano. The variations appear in contrasting guises, and the movement ends quietly.

The brief but fervent Allegro risoluto (D minor) opens with a lengthy piano statement. A passage that suggests the pealing of funeral bells introduces the violin and cello. Numerous tempo changes dramatize the dialogue among the three instruments. The movement ends softly to suggest the calm acceptance of fate.

ELEVEN

Interludes in Italy and Spain: Boccherini, Rossini, Verdi, Puccini, Respighi, Falla, Turina

The cradle of opera during the Baroque era and long the well-spring for innovations in all genres, Italy over the centuries has made enormous contributions to both vocal and instrumental music. Yet from the eighteenth century onward Italy's production of chamber music has been modest—most probably because of steady demand for either large-scale theatrical works or small-scale duos and solos for aristocratic entertainment. A similar situation existed in Spain. Influenced by foreign visitors-in-residence such as Luigi Boccherini, Spain during the early nineteenth century nurtured classically oriented composers of chamber music such as the short-lived Juan Crisóstomo Arriaga (1806–1826). However, the extreme popular success of classical guitarist Fernando Sor (1778–1839) led Spain to focus on the possibilities of that instrument. Solo works for guitar and large genres such as the theatrical *zarzuela* prevailed. Only in the early part of the twentieth century did composers such as Turina resume composition of chamber music.

Italy's three most important operatic figures—Rossini, Verdi, and Puccini—explored chamber music as a diversion, and their unique contributions are discussed in this chapter together with Respighi, an instrumental composer with operatic concepts. Boccherini belongs both to Italy and to Spain, where he spent the majority of his career. Spain's three most significant composers—Albéniz, Granados, and Falla—wrote little chamber music, but one can treasure Falla's Chamber Concerto for Harpsichord as a rare example.

LUIGI BOCCHERINI
B. FEBRUARY 19, 1743 IN LUCCA, ITALY,
D. MAY 28, 1805 IN MADRID

Guitar Quintet No. 4 in D Major, G. 448
("Fandango")

Pastorale
Allegro maestoso
Grave assai—Fandango

Although overshadowed by his contemporaries Haydn and Mozart, Luigi Boccherini is recognized as a creative figure whose elegantly ornamented works epitomize the graceful rococo spirit of the eighteenth century. Once unfortunately described as "Haydn's wife," Boccherini has been criticized for developing his incomparable melodies with greater simplicity than the Viennese classicists. However, Boccherini's persistent quest for new sonorities and his exploration of diverse instrumental combinations have significantly advanced chamber literature. Boccherini spent the majority of his career in Madrid, where he served as resident court composer and performer for Don Luis, brother of King Charles III of Spain. For his employment he produced many chamber compositions, among which are two forms that he pioneered: over 100 string quintets, mostly scored for two cellos, and the piano quintet genre, a string quartet combined with piano. Influenced by Spain's strong guitar tradition, he rescored nine of these piano or cello quintets for guitar and string quartet.

Boccherini quarried the opening movements of the popular Guitar Quintet "Fandango" (1798) from two earlier D major string quintets—G. 270 (1771) and G. 341 (1788)—and rescored them for guitar quintet. The superb "Fandango" finale was newly composed for the quintet.

The opening Pastorale reveals the fanciful lyric invention always evident in Boccherini's slower movements, which steadily evolved toward Romanticism. The Allegro maestoso features a prominent cello part that Boccherini (who owned a 1709 Stradivarius cello) would have relished as a performer.

A brief introduction marked Grave assai ("somewhat slow and serious") launches the exciting "Fandango" finale, a set of variations on an Andalusian folk melody. The fandango's strong and distinctive descending chord pattern (G minor-F major-E flat major-D major) recurs throughout. Often performed as a dramatic courtship dance, the fandango is traditionally accompanied by guitar, castanets, and handclaps. Its performers observe that the sensual fandango exhibits the voluptuousness of its gypsy origins.

GIOACHINO ROSSINI
B. FEBRUARY 29, 1792 IN PESARO, ITALY,
D. NOVEMBER 13, 1868 IN PARIS

String Sonata No. 6 in D Major for Two Violins, Cello, and Bass

Allegro spiritoso
Andante assai
Tempesta: Allegro

Europe's most celebrated opera composer in his maturity, Rossini wrote all of his chamber music during his early youth. His six string quartets were originally known as "Sonate a Quattro" (sonatas for four) but were freely transcribed for varying sizes of string and wind groups. Their manuscript, discovered in 1951, states that these "sonatas for four" were written in 1804, at which time their author was twelve years old. At that time the Rossini family lodged with a double bass player who enjoyed performing chamber music, and the precocious composer scored his "sonatas" to include him. In 1825 Rossini revised and published the works, now renamed as quartets.

Rossini admired all classical masters, but Mozart provided the primary model for his quartets. Rossini stated: "I listen to Mozart each day. He is always so enchanting." Like Mozart's quartets, each of Rossini's quartets features songful melodic lines, and virtuoso execution is required of all players. Each instrument performs an independent line; the cello and bass are not paired on similar parts, as was customary. Although Rossini's first choice of the word "sonata" for these early chamber works implies adherence to sonata form, his treatment of this classical structure is rudimentary, especially in the opening allegro movements. His genius lay with delightful narrative, and these early works develop with a "buffa" quality that anticipates his mature operatic style.

The opening Allegro spiritoso develops with clear phrasing, inventive scoring, and an overall good-natured atmosphere. The Andante assai (F major) is a lyrical song that suggests the influence of Mozart. The quartet's expressive core is its Allegro finale, the "Tempesta" (storm)—a free fantasia that anticipates the storm section heard in his Overture to *William Tell*. The movement opens with a suggestion of cheerful bird song in the violins; gradually the storm gathers, heard in the ever more furious scale figurations. Tranquility returns at the quiet conclusion.

GIUSEPPE VERDI
B. OCTOBER 10, 1813 IN LE RONCOLE, ITALY,
D. JANUARY 27, 1901 IN MILAN

String Quartet in E Minor

Allegro
Andantino
Prestissimo
Scherzo Fuga: Allegro assai mosso

During the frustrating period when the Naples premiere of *Aida* was continually postponed due to the leading soprano's illness, Verdi wrote his only chamber composition, the String Quartet in E Minor (1873). The work was premiered at a surprise concert for close friends who were impressed that Italy's greatest opera composer could find time for chamber music. Although Verdi initially discouraged both publication and further performances, the quartet has endured in the repertoire because of its fine melodies and fluent string writing.

The E minor Quartet develops with technically demanding passagework for all instruments and an abundance of quasi-operatic ideas. The opening Allegro's first theme suggests the melodic figure associated with Amneris in *Aida*. A contemplative second subject provides a quiet contrast. The Andantino, which Verdi said should be played "with elegance," is a rondo with three appearances of a graceful theme separated by two contrasting episodes. The fast and energetic Prestissimo features in its middle section an aria for cello with the guitar-like accompaniment of the other strings. The high-spirited finale is based on a single subject that is ingeniously varied and developed fugally, with all instruments imitating the ideas in sequence. The coda, marked "a little bit faster," brings the work to a vibrant conclusion.

GIACOMO PUCCINI
B. DECEMBER 22, 1858 IN LUCCA, ITALY,
D. NOVEMBER 29, 1924 IN BRUSSELS

Crisantemi for String Quartet

The foremost Italian operatic composer after Verdi, Giacomo Puccini is known for writing fervently lyrical works imbued with tenderness and gentle melancholy. A creator of fragile heroines memorable for their vulnerability and the nobility of their love, he confessed that he was not temperamentally suited for dramas on a Wagnerian scale: "The only music I can make is of small things," he wrote. His sensitive operatic style earned early recognition with a La Scala production of *Edgar* in 1889, and he soon began drafts of *Manon Lescaut* (1893), his first international success.

Puccini wrote *Crisantemi* ("Chrysanthemums," 1890) while his later operatic triumphs were in progress conceptually. The title refers to the elegant yet durable flower that was a favorite memorial at Italian funerals. The Duke Amadeo d'Aosta had suddenly died, and within the space of an evening Puccini wrote his elegy for string quartet as a tribute to his aristocratic supporter. Later, *Crisantemi* provided source material for both the prison window and death scenes in the third act of *Manon Lescaut*. An expressive, sustained andante movement in C sharp minor, the work develops with affecting chromaticism and subtle changes of tempo.

OTTORINO RESPIGHI
B. JULY 9, 1879 IN BOLOGNA,
D. APRIL 18, 1936 IN ROME

Piano Quintet in F Minor, P. 35

Allegro
Andantino
Vivacissimo

Because his works were championed by Toscanini, Ottorino Respighi became one of the most famous Italian composers of the early twentieth century. Respighi has often been compared to his literary contemporary, the author Gabriele d'Annunzio, because of his lyrically fluent and sensuous modes of expression. Respighi is best known for his early symphonic poems *The Pines of Rome* and *The Fountains of Rome*, lavish programmatic works that develop with brilliant instrumental color. Yet Respighi sought more than the grand effect. Rigorously trained in various European capitals, he admired the nuanced harmonies of Debussy and Strauss. Always devoted to early music, Respighi intended to invigorate his compositions through musical gestures derived from ancient Italian roots and Gregorian chant.

Respighi wrote his Piano Quintet (1902) while he studied with the Russian nationalist composer Rimsky-Korsakov in St. Petersburg. An atmospheric work, Respighi's Quintet reveals poetically muted passages and occasional moments of melancholy. Evocative details, such as depictions of tolling bells, reflect his impressions of Russia.

The Quintet opens with a unison statement of the main theme played by the four strings. The piano answers with a second motif. The movement then develops its ideas episodically through a wide range of dynamics and changes of key. The brief Andantino (B flat minor) is cast in three-part song form with a central interlude for piano. The Vivacissimo, which follows without pause, opens with a playful figure in the piano smoothly answered by the strings (B flat major). After a substantial interlude featuring the piano, the Andantino returns (B flat minor). The tempo then accelerates and the work concludes with a prestissimo flourish.

MANUEL DE FALLA
B. NOVEMBER 23, 1876 IN CADIZ, SPAIN,
D. NOVEMBER 14, 1946 IN ALTA GRACIA, ARGENTINA

Concerto for Harpsichord, Flute, Oboe, Clarinet, Violin, and Cello

Allegro
Lento (Giubiloso ed energico)
Vivace (Flessibile, scherzando)

Like his compatriots Granados and Albéniz, Manuel de Falla credited his teacher Felipe Pedrell for instilling the native Iberian spirit that infuses his compositions. Pedrell, also a composer, gave his students insights into the deepest roots of Spanish music, a venerable tradition that predates the gypsy elements often associated with it. Later, during his seven years in Paris, Falla befriended Debussy and Ravel, and the three composers were mutually influential.

Attracted to the harpsichord because of its tonal resemblance to the Spanish guitar, Falla wrote his chamber concerto (1923, completed in 1926) for Wanda Landowska, who had rescued the keyboard instrument from oblivion. A rugged and austere work, the concerto showcases the particular sonority of the harpsichord, which at moments evokes the sound of the guitar.

Although constructed according to classical principles, the concerto reflects the influence of Stravinsky, particularly in its polytonal (two keys heard simultaneously) outer movements. Of these, the opening Allegro develops a fifteenth-century Spanish song, *De los álamos vengo, Madre* ("I come from the poplar trees, Mother") and the concluding Vivace moves with joyous dance rhythms. The emotional center of the work lies in the remarkable Lento, which bears Falla's inscription as an expression of faith: "In the year of the Lord 1926, on Corpus Christi Day." This deeply mystical and concentrated movement is intended to be heard and felt as a tonal prayer.

JOAQUÍN TURINA
B. DECEMBER 9, 1882 IN SEVILLE,
D. JANUARY 14, 1949 IN MADRID

Piano Quartet in A Minor, Opus 67

Lento—Andante mosso
Vivo
Andante—Allegretto

Iberian composer Joaquín Turina was born and raised in Seville. His father Joaquín was a noted painter of Andalusian genre scenes, and most probably he influenced his musical son to think descriptively as he composed. After abandoning early medical studies, the younger Turina moved to Madrid, where he met Manuel de Falla and with him resolved to create musical portraits of Spanish life. Like Falla, Turina spent several formative years in Paris, where he enrolled at the Schola Cantorum and studied with French romanticist Vincent d'Indy, a close follower of César Franck. After his return to Spain, Turina achieved popular success with works based on traditional Sevillian and Andalusian themes. Despite difficulties during the Spanish Civil War, when his family fell out of favor with the Republicans, Turina pursued an honored career as Professor of Composition at the Madrid Conservatory. His collected works number over one hundred symphonic, chamber, vocal, and piano compositions.

Turina's lyrical Piano Quartet (1931) is a work of warm sonorities and subtle elegance that shows the influence of César Franck in its pervasive cyclic structure, a means of unifying the movements through a recall of themes. The three movements, arranged in a traditional fast-slow-fast scheme, all suggest the grace and vitality of popular Spanish folk dance and song. Each movement develops freely with moments of declamation that reflect the improvisational singing style of the Spanish gypsies. Opulent instrumental color enlivens the entire work.

The Quartet's introduction states the fervent main theme, a flowing Iberian-influenced melody that recurs throughout all movements. Florid melodies in the strings overlay rich chromatic figuration in the piano, directed to be played "in a singing style." Numerous changes of tempo, texture, and dynamics lend drama to this atmospheric movement.

The rapid, triple-time Vivo is based on a *jota*, a vigorous dance of northern Spain. Pizzicato passages suggest the lively interplay of guitars. The main theme of the first movement, underpinned by modal harmonies, is quoted at its center.

As in the Quartet's opening, a brief introduction (Andante) prefaces the finale. The Allegretto's two expressive themes shift through a variety of changing tempos; sonorous blocks of harmony progress in parallel motion to suggest the impressionist influence of Debussy. A rapturous statement of the main theme concludes the work.

TWELVE

Diversity in Fin-de-siècle France: Franck, Chaminade, Saint-Saëns, Fauré, Chausson, Debussy, Ravel

French chamber music flourished during the first fifty years of the Third Republic (1870–1940), a time of artistic and scientific achievement nurtured by a government that had miraculously survived numerous strains and scandals such as the Dreyfus Affair. Characterized by energetic diversity, French chamber style at that time accommodated differing tastes and temperaments— evidenced by the nineteen chamber concert series offered in Paris. The late romantic sensibilities of Franck, Chaminade, Saint-Saëns, Fauré, and Chausson elevated the medium above its often-perceived role as dance accompaniment, and the forward-looking creations of Debussy and Ravel brought French chamber music into the modern era. It is notable that the important composers and performers of this time were trained in France rather than Germany, a new phenomenon that contributed to the creation of a national French voice.

CÉSAR FRANCK
B. DECEMBER 10, 1822 IN LIÈGE, BELGIUM,
D. NOVEMBER 8, 1890 IN PARIS

Piano Quintet in F Minor, FWV 7

Molto moderato quasi lento—Allegro
Lento, con molto sentimento
Allegro non troppo, ma con fuoco

The Franco-Belgian composer and organist César Franck wrote one piano quintet, a work that stands apart from his other compositions because of its heightened drama and passion. Friends of the placid composer, who normally created serene and ethereal compositions, expressed shock at the fervor of this Quintet. They suspected that its tempestuousness grew from Franck's obvious infatuation with his red-haired Irish student at the conservatory, the beautiful Augusta Holmès (later immortalized in a portrait by Renoir).

The Quintet's premiere in 1879 was a disaster. Franck, never fond of detailed rehearsals, had asked his colleague Camille Saint-Saëns to sight-read the massive piano part. The audience watched in fascination as Saint-Saëns, who also admired Augusta, grew repelled to the point of nausea by the strong passions evident in the score. At the work's conclusion, Franck attempted to present Saint-Saëns, the dedicatee, with a copy of the manuscript. Saint-Saëns refused the gesture and stalked offstage. Madame Franck, aware of her rival in the audience, showed disgust as well.

The Quintet achieves drama in part through its extreme range of dynamics, which move impetuously from fortissississimo (very, very loud) to pianississimo (very, very soft). A tightly unified work, the Quintet's three movements all develop in sonata form. The first and third movements begin with full introductions and conclude with passionate codas as a summary of ideas. Of special importance is the second theme heard in the first movement, a motto marked "sweetly with passion" in which intervals pull toward and away from a pivotal note to suggest yearning. This idea is developed in each of the movements to create a cyclical form.

CÉCILE CHAMINADE
B. AUGUST 8, 1857 IN PARIS,
D. APRIL 13, 1944 IN MONACO

Piano Trio in G Minor, Opus 11

Allegro
Andante
Presto
Allegro molto

A child prodigy, French pianist and composer Cécile Chaminade wrote her first compositions at age eight, and by the age of sixteen she was already a successful concert pianist. One of the first women to make a career of composing, she produced over 200 lyrical, finely crafted works. Chaminade has been described erroneously as a composer of charming salon pieces—but her substantial output includes two piano trios, a choral symphony, and the virtuoso Opus 40 Concertstück. Chaminade's delicate and imaginative compositions exude a late romantic atmosphere within essentially classical structures.

The Trio in G Minor, Opus 11 (ca. 1880) opens with a graceful Allegro written in clear sonata form. The serene Andante presents melodic passages for strings underpinned by reiterated piano chords that sustain the harmony. Presto, marked "light and fast," moves with a deftness that suggests the scherzo movements of Mendelssohn. The work concludes with a vivacious Allegro molto.

CAMILLE SAINT-SAËNS
B. OCTOBER 9, 1835 IN PARIS,
D. DECEMBER 16, 1921 IN ALGIERS

Septet in E flat Major for String Quartet, Double Bass,
Trumpet, and Piano, Opus 65

Préambule: Allegro moderato
Menuet: Tempo di minuetto moderato
Intermède: Andante
Gavotte et Finale: Allegro non troppo

A musician of extraordinary versatility, Camille Saint-Saëns continuously experimented with new sonorities in his chamber works. Obsessed with clarity and precision, he also sought formal perfection even as he realized that his individual style of classicized romanticism would soon be outmoded. As early as 1879 he perhaps anticipated his future compatriot Olivier Messiaen: "Tonality is in its death throes. There will be an eruption of the Oriental modes, whose variety is immense. Rhythm, scarcely exploited, will be developed. From all this will emerge a new art."

Saint-Saëns wrote his Opus 65 Septet (1880) at the request of "La Trompette," a Parisian musical society that desired a chamber work emphasizing the trumpet for its Christmas celebration. Initially skeptical of the project, he told the director: "I will write you a concerto for twenty-five guitars and to perform it you will have to depopulate Andalusia; but chamber music with trumpet—it's impossible!" Nevertheless, he did write the Septet in time for its scheduled premiere, and the work was received as one of his finest chamber music compositions. Constructed in the form of an eighteenth-century suite—a set of stylized dance movements prefaced by an introduction—the work develops a military character because of its direct quotations of a French army regimental call.

The Septet combines the baroque influence of Handel (heard

especially in its fugal passages) with moments of songful romanticism. Its Préambule introduces a vigorous theme that pervades
the work; quieter moments anticipate themes from the following
movements. Three contrasting themes alternate in the crisply energetic Menuet. The Intermède is a somber march underpinned by a
pervasive dactylic rhythm (long-short-short) in the accompanying
voices. Piano acrobatics predominate in the dancelike Gavotte,
which ends brilliantly with a flourish of military calls.

GABRIEL FAURÉ
B. MAY 12, 1845 IN POITIERS, FRANCE,
D. NOVEMBER 4, 1924 IN PARIS

Piano Quartet in G Minor, Opus 45

Allegro molto moderato
Allegro molto
Adagio non troppo
Allegro molto

Perhaps motivated by the encouraging environment for chamber arts in Paris, the French romanticist Gabriel Fauré created
significant instrumental works together with an exquisite body of
songs. Poetic expressions of his own personal vision, these compositions convey his mystical concept of beauty through a subtle and
sensuous harmonic palette.

Often regarded as his finest chamber work, the G Minor Piano
Quartet was written in 1886, the same year Fauré composed his
masterful Requiem. Whereas in his earlier chamber works Fauré
had closely followed classical French models of form and harmony,
in Opus 45 he outlines a romantically bold design enlivened by
unexpected discords. The work develops as a surging flow of wide-
ly-arched lyrical themes supported by dynamic figuration in the

accompaniment.

The opening movement integrates programmatic autobiographical motifs into the thematic material. Fauré's childhood was cherished but brief (he was sent to boarding school in Paris at age nine), and auditory imagery from his earliest years permeates his work. He wrote that the fervent first theme evokes the forge sounds he heard as a youth, and the movement's "tranquillamente" sections (E flat major) evoke his childhood experience of the Angelus, a daily call to prayer accompanied by the pealing of a bell.

In the rapid Allegro molto the meter playfully changes from patterns of three note groups to two. This alternation creates an animated underpinning for the melody, a broad restatement of the first movement's opening theme. Fauré here omits the central trio section customary for scherzo movements to create a compact form.

The Adagio non troppo, one of Fauré's most poetic movements, is cast in A-B-A song form. Gently undulating rhythmic patterns suggest a barcarolle, a boatman's song. Subtly varied thematic statements in the strings are supported by rich harmonies to create a full, sonorous texture.

The rhapsodic finale develops two themes with unexpected changes of harmony. As in the second movement, an alternation of duple and triple metric patterns energizes the rhythm. Motifs from Fauré's childhood return; forceful and repetitive piano figuration at the center conjures the image of the town forge. Near its conclusion the mode shifts from minor to major to suggest positive resolution for this occasionally autobiographical work.

ERNEST CHAUSSON
B. JANUARY 20, 1855 IN PARIS,
D. JUNE 10, 1899 IN LIMAY, FRANCE

Piano Trio in G Minor, Opus 3

Pas trop lent—Animé
Vite
Assez lent
Animé

French romanticist Ernest Chausson wrote his early G Minor Piano Trio in 1881, the formative year in which he left his mentor Jules Massenet to study with César Franck. Franck's celebrated Piano Quintet had been premiered the previous year, and Chausson's first chamber work, the Opus 3, could hardly escape its passionate and dramatic aura. Certainly Chausson knew the direction his own work must take, for his friends observed that he created the trio in his mind before writing down any notes. His fellow composer d'Indy wrote, "Chausson belongs to that strong race that suffers through their idea before producing it."

A brief introduction, Pas trop lent (not too slow), leads to a faster section marked Animé (animated). Essentially monothematic, this restless movement develops with numerous abrupt dynamic changes, a similarity to Franck's Quintet. Unsettled chromatic lines heard throughout the movement create an agitated atmosphere.

Vite (fast) is an intermezzo that develops with wit and poise. Its short phrases, each of three or four measures duration, are structured with an ear to symmetry. Double stops in the violin (two notes played at once) create a full harmonic texture.

The third movement, Assez lent (rather slow), expands the theme of the first movement to create a plaintive but sonorous statement. Each instrument precisely articulates its own elegiac line, all of which blend to form an expressive unity.

The vibrant Animé contains echoes of earlier themes; this hint of cyclic construction suggests the influence of Chausson's new mentor, Franck. The vivid themes and rhythms of this movement, as well as its overall solid craftsmanship, led d'Indy to write: "One feels, amid the Trio's beauties and weaknesses, the still unrealized aspirations of his soul and the foreshadowing of future works."

Piano Quartet in A Major, Opus 30

Animé
Andante
Simple et sans hâte
Animé

Ernest Chausson has been described as the late romantic link between César Franck, his teacher and continuing mentor, and Claude Debussy, his close friend. During his early years, Chausson created lushly textured works with elegant, fluent melodies that suggest the operatic arias of Jules Massenet, his stylistically influential Paris Conservatory professor. Fond of French Symbolist poetry and Russian novels, Chausson established a salon, and his literary friends encouraged him to compose with heightened drama. After the death of his father, Chausson moved toward a subtler impressionistic style with clear and skillfully crafted lines. Chausson himself died five years later at age 44 after a bicycle accident—while riding downhill on his pre-safety cycle, he lost control of his contraption and crashed into a brick wall. At the time of his early death, Chausson had earned a solid reputation as a composer of both operas and instrumental works. He created six chamber compositions, all works of refined lyric poetry that significantly contribute to the repertoire.

Chausson began his Opus 30 in the spring of 1897 and premiered it that same year. The work blends serene classicism with rhapsodic lyricism. The opening movement, animated by alternating rhythmic patterns, develops two themes based on the pentatonic scale (five notes per octave). The eloquent Andante (D flat major) develops an extended theme that evokes alternately pathos and reverie. The dancelike third movement, "simple and without haste," is a light and elegant scherzo based on a melody suggesting Spanish folksong. The bravura finale, remarkable in its rhythmic flexibility, recalls themes from the earlier movements to create a cyclic form. The quartet concludes with a passionate recapitulation of the lyrical theme heard in the second movement.

CLAUDE DEBUSSY

B. AUGUST 22, 1862 AT SAINT-GERMAIN-EN-LAYE, FRANCE,
D. MARCH 25, 1918 IN PARIS

String Quartet in G Minor, Opus 10

Animé et très décidé
Assez vif et bien rythmé
Andantino, doucement expressif
Très modéré

Musical impressionism flowered with Claude Debussy, who in the 1890s continued the movement generated twenty years earlier by the painter Monet and the symbolist poet Mallarmé. Debussy sought to impart a similarly ineffable atmosphere by emphasizing color and nuance rather than systematic thematic development. He achieved his sensitive and haunting style through brief melodies, often based on ancient or exotic scales, supported by shifting harmonies and rapidly changing meters.

An early work, the Quartet in G Minor (1893) reveals both established techniques and evidence of Debussy's revolutionary new language. Its movements conform to traditional sonata, scherzo, and three-part song form structures. The influence of his older contemporary César Franck can be heard in the quartet's cyclic form—a unifying device in which related thematic material permeates all movements. Yet the quartet's evocative sonorities anticipate the fully impressionistic world Debussy created in his next work, *Prélude à l'après-midi d'un faune* ("Prelude to The Afternoon of a Faun," 1894).

Kaleidoscopic permutations of this material recur throughout the entire quartet. The second movement, a piquant scherzo animated by colorful pizzicato figures, led César Franck to observe that "Debussy creates music on needle points." At the 1889 Paris Exposition a Javanese gamelan orchestra had enchanted Debussy, and his contemporary critics heard similarly exotic effects in this scherzo.

The third movement, cast in three-part song form, is framed by a passionate song for muted strings; a lyrical episode for viola and cello falls at its center. The finale opens with a quiet introduction and accelerates with a fugato section based on the quartet's opening theme. This agile movement inventively synthesizes material from the preceding three movements. It concludes with a brilliant coda.

MAURICE RAVEL
B. MARCH 7, 1875 IN CIBOURE, FRANCE,
D. DECEMBER 28, 1937 IN PARIS

String Quartet in F Major, M. 35

Allegro moderato—Très doux
Assez vif—Très rythmé
Très lent
Vif et agité

Ravel composed his only string quartet while he was affiliated as a student auditor at the Paris Conservatory in 1903–4. Two years previously he had been expelled from the formal program because of his unwillingness to write fugues: however, Gabriel Fauré continued to welcome Ravel to his composition class. Ravel dedicated his F Major Quartet to Fauré and with his encouragement submitted its first movement to the Prix de Rome jury. Three times previously the jury, comprised primarily of conservatory professors, had rejected Ravel's application for this important prize, which included several years of financial support. In his latest attempt Ravel was eliminated in the first round—an outrage that touched off a scandal in the artistic community.

Controversy continued to surround the F Major Quartet after its official 1904 premiere. Critics heard striking parallels to Debussy's Quartet in G Minor (1893), which in fact had been a model, and comparisons were much discussed. The publicity angered Debussy, with whom Ravel had been on cordial terms, and caused a breach between the two composers. Ironically, it was Debussy who bestowed the highest praise on the new quartet. When Ravel asked for his opinion of the quartet, Debussy replied: "In the name of the gods of music, and in mine, do not touch a single note of what you have written in your quartet."

Although Ravel's quartet was undeniably influenced by Debussy, the new work is essentially different because of its clearer structure. Unlike Debussy, who strove to express the ineffable through a subtly nuanced mosaic of themes, Ravel grounds his quartet with clearly cadenced phrases. Yet Debussy's influence is heard in Ravel's free harmonic language and in his exploration of instrumental color. Like Debussy, Ravel was influenced by Far Eastern music, and one hears in his work a similar Javanese influence.

The Quartet in F Major is a cyclic work in which material heard in the opening movement recurs in the third and fourth movements to unify the structure. The lyrical opening movement, Allegro moderato, is based on two themes developed with classical poise. Like the second movement of Debussy's quartet, Ravel's "Rather lively" second movement conjures the image of a Javanese gamelan orchestra. The first theme is played pizzicato in the Aeolian mode (corresponding to an octave of piano white keys beginning on A); the serene second theme provides contrast. The colorful and rhapsodic third movement ("Very slow") interweaves themes from the first movement with new material. The vigorous finale, "Lively and agitated," alternates tremolo passages in quintuple meter with songful triple-meter passages derived from the first movement. A brief reprise of the movement's opening material and a passage of ascending thirds bring the work to a brilliant conclusion.

Piano Trio in A Minor, M. 67

Modéré
Pantoum: Assez vif
Passacaille: Très large
Final: Animé

In February 1914 Ravel left Paris to be near his mother in St. Jean-de-Luz, a small Basque village near the Spanish border. He planned to work on two projects—a piano concerto incorporating Basque themes and a piano trio—but abandoned plans for the concerto and incorporated its themes, which he described as "Basque in color," into the trio's first movement.

Composition proceeded well until the outbreak of World War I, which coincided with initial work on the finale. Ravel was eager to serve in the military, and in fact later became an ambulance driver for the French army. Yet he was reluctant to leave his aged mother. He wrote to a friend: "If you only knew how I am suffering. If I leave my poor old mother it will surely kill her. But so as not to think of this, I am working with the sureness and lucidity of a madman." Because of his feverish pace, this work was soon completed. With its brilliant writing, wide range of instrumental color, and refined elegance, the Piano Trio is considered to be one of Ravel's finest compositions.

The first movement explores Spanish rhythms and melodies with French gracefulness. Its two themes are based on a popular Basque folk dance with a persistent 3-2-3 rhythm. After a brief development, the movement concludes as a fragment of the opening theme fades into a rhythmic outline tapped in the piano's low register.

Ravel entitled the scherzo movement *Pantoum*, a Malay poetic form in which the second and fourth lines of one stanza become the first and third of the next. Its rapid rhythms, pizzicati, and harmonics create a dazzling effect. In the middle section the strings continue their brilliant passage work in a fast 3/4 meter while the piano articulates contrasting chorale-like phrases in 4/2 time.

The clear melodic contours, distinct rhythms, and lucid structure of the third movement, a passacaglia, suggest Ravel's classical orientation. Ten variations of its opening theme are arranged in arch form. The statements begin quietly and gradually gain fervor, then calm as the movement approaches its conclusion.

The energetic Animé, following without pause, opens with fortissimo repeated violin arpeggios. The primary theme, related to the principal theme of the first movement, is heard in the piano. Virtuosic trills, arpeggios, and tremolos propel the movement toward its exhilarating conclusion on a high A major chord.

THIRTEEN

A Flowering in Post-Victorian England: Bridge, Vaughan Williams, Elgar, Britten

Although Great Britain produced outstanding composers before 1700 and remained an unparalleled source of both literary genius and influential thinkers since the early Renaissance, it reached a low ebb of distinguished music creation during much of the eighteenth and nineteenth centuries. This discrepancy was much observed. Robert Schumann, writing as a music critic, pronounced the British music scene "dismal," and the continent's curmudgeon, Belgian music critic François-Joseph Fétis, complained that "music is dead there because the English cannot understand or appreciate it." (In fairness, an active concert life flourished in London due to foreign visitors such as Mendelssohn.) The young Vaughan Williams objected vehemently to the stifled quality he detected in his nation's music. He wrote: "Away with good taste! What we want in England is real music, even if it be only a music-hall song. Provided it possesses real feeling and real life, it will be worth all the classics in the world." Only near the end of Queen Victoria's reign (1837–1901) did important compositions began to emerge, possibly because of the support from institutions such as the Royal Academy of Music. The diverse post-Victorian composers Bridge, Vaughan Williams, Elgar, and Britten, often inspired by England's great musical past, have revived the momentum of British composition.

FRANK BRIDGE
B. FEBRUARY 26, 1879 IN BRIGHTON,
D. JANUARY 10, 1941 IN EASTBOURNE, UK

String Quartet in E Minor, H. 70 ("Bologna")

Adagio—Allegro appassionato
Adagio molto
Allegretto grazioso—Allegro vivace
Allegro agitato

The music of Frank Bridge fell into neglect after his death, but his masterfully crafted and poetic works are currently undergoing revival. The composition teacher of Benjamin Britten, who honored him by incorporating Bridge themes into his own works, Bridge has been called a "musician's musician" because of his outstanding competence as a violinist, conductor, and composer with a subtle understanding of instrumental color. Bridge studied violin and composition at the Royal College of Music under the tutelage of Charles Stanford, a difficult taskmaster notorious for discouraging all but the strongest candidates. After graduation Bridge joined the English String Quartet as violinist. He then composed both substantial, warmly romantic chamber works as well as light, entertaining pieces that unjustly contributed to his reputation as a salon composer. Benjamin Britten defended Bridge: "When Frank Bridge matured at the turn of the century, the school of chamber music was in the doldrums. Bridge was not only a listener and composer but a player too. Little wonder he wanted to write music grateful to play and easy to listen to."

Bridge wrote his String Quartet No. 1 (1901) for a competition held by the Accademia Filarmonica in Bologna, and it won the Honorable Mention award. Already an experienced chamber composer with several works to his credit, including an early string quartet without an opus number, Bridge composed his large-scale

E Minor String Quartet within a month. This new quartet reveals his affinity to Brahms's romanticism but also offers hints of the early impressionism heard in Debussy's String Quartet in G Minor, a work that Bridge had recently discovered.

The Quartet begins with a brief introduction as the cello softly states the first theme. The passionate Allegro that follows without pause develops two new themes with fervor and sweep. Rich harmonies create a colorful late romantic sound world. A calmer second thematic area (G major) introduces sweetly expressive themes that evoke the fin-de-siècle atmosphere of the salon. The opening themes return and are recapitulated "with warmth." The movement concludes with an emphatic coda.

The second movement, in A-B-A form, consists of two related Adagio statements that frame a faster contrasting central section. Reflective soliloquys vary the expressive themes of the outer sections; soft dynamics and calm tempos create a gentle affect.

The Allegretto grazioso is a delicate scherzo that unfolds like a graceful dance. A variation of the first movement's primary theme returns in the contrasting central section.

The dramatic finale develops two energetic motifs with florid textures punctuated by solo soliloquys. Themes from the opening movement are recalled, and all ideas are expansively stated. The movement ends quietly with a cello allusion to the first movement's introduction.

Piano Quintet in D Minor, H. 49

Adagio—Allegro moderato
Adagio ma non troppo—Allegro con brio—
    Adagio ma non troppo
Allegro energico

Bridge's early Piano Quintet reveals influences of both Brahms and Debussy, whose G Minor String Quartet was a personal favorite. In 1904–5 Bridge crafted the Quintet's massive first version, a large-proportioned four-movement work with a virtuoso piano score. After two discouraging performances, Bridge filed the work in a drawer. In 1912 he revised the Quintet substantially—the angular first movement was replaced by a more impressionist statement; the second and third movements were condensed into a symmetrical arch; the finale was abbreviated. Much of the complex piano writing was simplified. The Quintet's new version was described as a "revelation" by its listeners.

The Quintet begins with a quiet statement of the first theme by the violin and cello. At the Allegro moderato the solo viola articulates this idea, now twice as fast, against a flowing piano line. A crescendo leads to the emphatic second theme, stated by the unison strings, and the two ideas are enlarged with fervor and sweep. At the development muted pedal effects in the piano and triple-soft utterances in the strings conjure a mysterious atmosphere. The harmony grows more chromatic and the dynamics increase, culminating in a section marked "with passion." At a passage marked "little by little more tranquil" the tempo slows and the strings sing expressive lines based on the first theme. The opening tempo returns with a reprise of the first theme, developed "with warmth"; the mode changes to major at a passage marked "sweetly." Momentum subsides and the movement concludes with a hushed statement in D minor.

The second movement consists of two Adagio non troppo statements in B major with a contrasting central section in A minor (Allegro con brio). The first outer section explores two themes marked "sweetly and with expression." Soft dynamics and calm rallentandi create a gentle affect. The rapid central section is a scherzo that unfolds like a mischievous dance; staccato figuration adds piquancy. An ethereal cello soliloquy signals the return of the Adagio non troppo. Momentum builds and subsides, and the movement concludes quietly.

The dramatic finale (D minor) is propelled initially by short fragments exchanged between the strings and piano. As in the first movement two contrasting motifs are developed in passages alternately florid and spare. Themes from the first movement are recalled; the mode changes to D major and, as the tempo slows, all ideas are expansively stated. A tumultuous coda marked "with all force" concludes the movement.

RALPH VAUGHAN WILLIAMS
B. OCTOBER 12, 1872 IN DOWN AMPNEY, GLOUCESTERSHIRE,
D. AUGUST 26, 1958 IN LONDON

Quintet in C Minor for Piano, Violin, Viola, Cello, and Double Bass

Allegro con fuoco
Andante
Fantasia (quasi variazioni)

Ralph Vaughan Williams wrote numerous works admired for their "Englishness," a quality achieved through his deep assimilation of both British Isles folk song and the modalities heard in early English music. Acclaimed as the re-creator of his country's musical vernacular, Vaughan Williams earned a reputation as one of Europe's most distinctive musical personalities by the beginning of World War I. Yet he weathered a long and self-critical apprenticeship period. When Vaughan Williams wrote his early C Minor Quintet (1903), he already had composed four of his most famous songs and a cantata set to words by British poet Dante Gabriel Rosetti. But the Quintet's heavily marked and erased score reveals a new level of intense labor. Revised over the course of two years, the work was finally premiered in December 1905 by the finest musicians in London. Although successful performances followed, Vaughan Williams withdrew the work in 1918. He did not entirely repudiate its material since he quarried its Fantasia movement for themes developed in his 1954 violin sonata.

Vaughan Williams's early unpublished works all carry an embargo forbidding performance. However, because of intense interest in his music written before 1908, after a forty-year hiatus his widow Ursula agreed to the publication and performance of certain selected works, among which was the 1903 Quintet. Its first modern performance (1999) was held in London in association with the conference "Vaughan Williams in a New Century." In 2002 the Quintet was published by the British firm Faber Music Ltd.

Created for the same combination of instruments as Schubert's "Trout" Quintet (piano, violin, viola, cello, and double bass), the 1903 Quintet develops with the free Romanticism and fresh atmosphere characteristic of Vaughan Williams throughout his career. The tempestuous first movement offers strong contrasts of mood and dynamics. After extensive exploration of the opening lyrical theme, first heard in the viola (Vaughan Williams's favorite voice), an emphatic motive is played in unison by all instruments. This motto recurs in subsequent movements as a unifying device.

The Andante, marked to be played "tenderly," offers expressive interludes for the piano. After an agitated central section enhanced by remote harmonic excursions, the movement closes quietly with a muted string statement.

The Fantasia develops like the Elizabethan fantasy, a rhapsodic form that improvises on a principal motive. It opens with a soft unison statement of the theme, which is related to the strongly accented motto heard in the first movement. The five ensuing sections, designated as "almost variations" by Vaughan Williams, unfold with sharp contrasts of tempo, mood, and tonality. The movement closes in the same quiet atmosphere as its beginning.

Phantasy Quintet for Two Violins, Two Violas, and Cello

Prelude: Lento ma non troppo
Scherzo: Prestissimo
Alla Sarabanda: Lento
Burlesca: Allegro moderato

The Phantasy Quintet, completed in 1912, was commissioned by Walter Cobbett, the wealthy businessman and music lover who edited the pioneer *Cyclopedia for Chamber Music*. Cobbett especially admired Elizabethan fantasies, and he requested a work with similar rhapsodic improvisations on a theme. Vaughan Williams modelled his quintet on Henry Purcell's seventeenth-century viol fantasies, sectionalized works that unfold with maximum contrast of tempo and mood. To suggest the sound of the ancient viols, Vaughan Williams scored his work heavily for two violas. Written in four sections played without pause, all the movements are connected by the recurrent motto heard initially in the solo viola. His Phantasy (the original spelling) develops with clearly defined, seamless melodies that suggest improvised folk music.

A meditative Prelude, the first movement is based on a sinuous viola theme that outlines the pentatonic scale, the five-note framework that underpins much folk music. The vigorous Scherzo (Prestissimo) is propelled by an asymmetric meter, seven pulses to the bar. A legato cello figure leads to the poetic Alla Sarabanda. In a return to the reflective mood of the opening movement, the violins and violas engage in mysterious dialogue as the cello rests. The lively Burlesca suggests British folk dance. Momentum slows in the middle section as the solo viola quotes the theme of the opening Prelude. The work concludes with a calm and ethereal statement of the theme.

EDWARD ELGAR
B. JUNE 2, 1857 IN BROADHEATH, UK,
D. FEBRUARY 23, 1934 IN WORCESTER, UK

Piano Quintet in A Minor, Opus 84

Moderato—Allegro
Adagio
Andante—Allegro

A master of late romantic style, Edward Elgar contributed three important works to the chamber repertoire—a violin sonata, a string quartet, and his Opus 84 Piano Quintet. Elgar wrote all three works simultaneously beginning in 1918. His wife Alice had recently relocated the couple to a quiet cottage in Sussex, and Elgar, recovering from a throat operation, was delighted with its situation. Alice heard new sounds in the emerging works, the first chamber music that Elgar had written in thirty years—greater harmonic simplicity and an autumnal mood that she poetically described as "wood magic."

Elgar's property encompassed an eerily twisted group of white trees, a continual source of fascination for him. Local legend held that the trees were the ghosts of Spanish monks who had practiced black magic in the area. His literary interests at this time, encouraged by a visit from Algernon Blackwood, the noted author of truly terrifying horror tales, fueled his imagination. Elgar then requested that several novels of Edward Bulwer-Lytton (notorious for his opener "It was a dark and stormy night...") be sent to his remote cottage. Both he and Alice were enchanted by Bulwer-Lytton's "Strange Story," in which true love and witchcraft collide in an English village. Alice suggested the source of the Quintet's brooding atmosphere in a diary entry: "E. wrote more of the wonderful Quintet. Sad disposed trees and their dance and unstilled regret for their evil fate.... Lytton's 'Strange Story' seems to sound through it too."

World War I had entered its closing phase as Elgar began his Opus 84, and Elgar's deep concern for England's fate doubtless contributed to its unsettled atmosphere. A restless duality is heard throughout the work. Two themes continuously interweave—a somber motif based on plainchant that could be heard as the ominous beginning of a requiem mass; and a lilting theme that suggests the elegance and vivacity of Old Europe. In Opus 84 Elgar perhaps poses the question of whether or not the familiar order can continue.

The Quintet opens with an aura of mystery as the piano quietly intones the stark main theme in octaves ("serioso") and the strings utter a subdued accompaniment. The graceful second idea, which the violins play in thirds, resembles a Spanish dance theme. In the Allegro section, the two themes are recast and developed with symphonic richness. At the atmospheric conclusion, the strings and piano, now in low registers, engage in dramatic dialogue to create a sense of awe.

The three-part Adagio (E major) begins with a viola solo of poised elegance. The other strings join and interweave to create rich harmonies. Echoes of the opening movement themes return with variations; an elegiac motif is introduced by the first violin and answered by the cello. A calmly contrasting section (F major) features the viola, soon joined by the other strings. The original harmonies return (C sharp minor/E major) and the movement grows in fervency and sweep. The plainchant idea reappears and the movement closes in a hushed atmosphere.

The finale's Andante introduction reprises motifs from the opening movement. The ensuing Allegro develops two passionate themes in sonata form. Echoes of the first movement themes reappear and intertwine with these new ideas. A muted recapitulation of the nostalgic "Spanish" theme leads to the extended coda, which continuously accelerates until its "grandioso" conclusion.

BENJAMIN BRITTEN
B. NOVEMBER 22, 1913 IN LOWESTOFT, SUFFOLK,
D. DECEMBER 4, 1976 IN ALDEBURGH, SUFFOLK

Variations on a Theme of Frank Bridge, Opus 10

Introduction and Theme
Adagio
March
Romance
Aria Italiana
Bourrée Classique
Wiener Walzer
Moto perpetuo
Funeral March
Chant
Fugue and Finale

At age twenty-four Britten was invited to compose a work for the 1937 Salzburg Festival, a career-launching venue. He chose the theme for his projected composition from "Three Idylls for String Orchestra" by Frank Bridge, his first teacher. As a composer Britten, who was influenced by the great English traditions of choral music and the example of Henry Purcell, does not resemble Bridge, who looked to the continent for inspiration. Yet Bridge wrote compositions that Britten admired, for he recognized his mentor's remarkable feeling for the characters of the various instruments. Britten told Bridge that each of the variations revealed an aspect of his mentor's own character: integrity, energy, charm, humor, tradition, enthusiasm, vitality, sympathy, reverence, skill.

Bridge's strongly-profiled melodic theme, built on the intervals of the fourth and fifth, can be heard in each of the variations. Britten moves the theme to different voices to create contrasting moods. In the Funeral March, for example, the constructive interval of the fifth appears as an ostinato in the cellos and basses. Scored for string orchestra, the variations alternate in tempos and instrumental colors to create a dazzling and virtuosic whole.

String Quartet No. 2 in C Major, Opus 36

Allegro calmo senza rigore
Vivace
Chacony

In July, 1945 Britten and Yehudi Menuhin toured Germany as a piano and violin duo to perform for concentration camp survivors. Soon after his return, Britten wrote his String Quartet No. 2, a work ostensibly composed to commemorate the two hundred fiftieth anniversary of Henry Purcell's death but also one that testifies to the intensity of his recent experience. The quartet, perhaps his most popular chamber work, was completed in October, 1945 and premiered that November in London.

The quartet opens with calm statements of three melodious themes, each beginning with the wide interval of the tenth and accompanied by a sustained chord forming the interval of a tenth. An animato section leads to a quiet section with ghostly atmospheric effects created by glissandi and harmonics over sustained notes. At the "energico" development section tranquil and agitated passages alternate. The movement ends quietly with cello pizzicati punctuating ("like a harp") the softly sustained lines of the other instruments.

The Vivace movement (C minor) is a demonic scherzo that is no less ferocious because it is played with mutes throughout. Emphatic chords punctuate the opening section. In the contrasting trio section (F major) the first violin introduces a theme in long note values, an augmentation of the movement's primary theme.

The Chacony, a Tudor English respelling of the baroque "chaconne," pays homage to Purcell. The form consists of variations on a slow, triple-time ground, which here is a nine-measure melody initially played by the unison strings. The twenty-one variations that follow are separated into four groups by introductory cadenzas for the cello, viola, and first violin. Britten writes: "Each group explores a different aspect of the theme: harmonic, rhythmic, melodic, and formal. The final three variations together form a coda to the movement."

String Quartet No. 3 in G Major, Opus 94

Duets: With moderate movement
Ostinato: Very fast
Solo: Very calm
Burlesque: Fast, con fuoco
Recitative and Passacaglia (La Serenissima): Slow

In October, 1975 Britten began work on his third and final string quartet, a medium he had ignored for thirty years. Britten wrote this Opus 94 quartet for his longtime friends in the Amadeus Quartet and completed it during a November visit to Venice—the location perhaps inspiring incorporation of material from his 1973 opera *Death in Venice* into the last movement. Although Britten had the satisfaction of hearing the work in rehearsal, the Amadeus Quartet premiered the quartet a few days after his death.

Hans Keller, the work's dedicatee, states that in Quartet No. 3 "Britten ventures into the Mozartean realm of the instrumental purification of opera." Throughout his long career, Britten had placed highest value on the human voice, and portions of his final quartet develop with the direct simplicity of song. However, the quartet's first four movements also suggest the abstract modernist influence of Bartók and Shostakovich.

The opening movement, "Duets," develops six duo pairings centered on the interval of the second. "Ostinato," a scherzo movement, is based on a series of energetically syncopated intervals of the seventh. "Solo," the slow central movement, pays tribute to Amadeus quartet violinist Norbert Brainin. Its calm and ethereal melodic line is supported by triadic arpeggio figures for the other players. "Burlesque" combines sardonic humor with rhythmic drive.

"La Serenissima" offers themes from Britten's final opera, *Death in Venice*. The opening cello recitative recalls the barcarolle accompanying the Aschenbach's gondola rides. In the passacaglia section, important opera motifs are heard over the persistent ground bass. The work concludes, as Britten said, "with a question"—an ambiguous chord that denies full closure but conjures a still and serene atmosphere.

FOURTEEN

Bartók:
Quests and Transitions

BÉLA BARTÓK
B. MARCH 25, 1881 IN NAGYSZENTMIKLÓS, HUNGARY
(NOW ROMANIA), D. SEPTEMBER 26, 1945 IN NEW YORK CITY

————

STRING QUARTETS

————

From his rebellious student days Béla Bartók had longed to break away from Hapsburg Austria's Eurocentric cultural domination by creating, as he wrote, "something specifically Hungarian in music." While on a country outing in 1904 he happened to hear a young peasant girl singing an indigenous folk song, and his path became clear. Bartók and his colleague Zoltán Kodály packed their unwieldy recording equipment into a primitive truck and began to search out songs from Hungary's deep countryside. Their ethnomusicology quest resulted in an archive of over a thousand carefully catalogued songs and dances. Bartók intended to use this native material as the inspirational starting point for his original compositions: "It was not a question of taking unique melodies and incorporating them into our works. What we had to do was to divine the spirit of this unknown music and to make this spirit the basis for our own works." Bartók gradually assimilated the essences of these songs into his own musical thought processes. Much of the imaginative power of his six string quartets stems from his fusion of folk and art music.

Bartók wrote his monumental set of six string quartets during the years from 1909 to 1939, the core of his compositional career in Budapest before his emigration to the United States in 1940. Each quartet both marks the phases of his evolving creative development and serves as a diary of his emotional and intellectual life. These six string quartets, together with the fifteen quartets of Shostakovich, have been recognized as the most important contributions to the genre since the string quartets of Beethoven. Yet they remain demanding works for both listeners and interpreters, in part because of the lofty goal that Bartók set for their composition—to harness the instinctive, primitive forces inherent in his native Hungarian music with the most intellectually sophisticated aspects of the Western European string quartet genre.

String Quartet No. 1, Sz. 40

Lento
Allegretto
Introduzione: Allegro—Allegro vivace

Bartók completed his Opus 7 String Quartet No. 1 in 1909 during a period of intense romantic disappointment. His sympathetic friend and colleague Kodály called the quartet "an intimate drama, a return to life at the edge of nothing." Although influenced by the late romantic harmonic palette of Strauss and Wagner, Bartók in Quartet No. 1 began to forge a uniquely colorful style informed by native folk structures, expressively underpinned by blocks of modal harmony and propelling rhythms.

Strong thematic connections unify the movements. The Lento,

ternary in form, begins with a double canon based on two motifs that reappear in different guises throughout the quartet. After an agitated development of themes, the opening ideas are briefly recapitulated. The Allegretto is a scherzo that proceeds without pause. Its thematic material references the Lento but is constantly reshaped and developed in a rustic, playful manner. The movement begins with chromatically rising thirds in the cello and viola. A gradual acceleration leads to a lyrical countertheme underpinned by a propulsive ostinato, a repeating accompaniment figure.

The finale, Allegro vivace, is introduced by a cello recitative that mimics the rhythms of Magyar speech—which typically emphasizes the first syllables of the words and falls into a short-long accent pattern. The main thematic area, derived from motives in the first two movements, suggests a vigorous folk dance. A slower section based on the Hungarian melody "The Peacock Flies" recalls the opening double canon of the Lento. Energy rebuilds and the movement concludes with a joyous spirit.

String Quartet No. 2, Sz. 67

Moderato
Allegro molto capriccioso
Lento

Because of the difficult circumstances created by World War I, the composition of his Opus 17 Quartet No. 2 extended over a two-year period (1915–1917). Bartók described the work's unusual structure: "I cannot undertake an analysis of the form—there is nothing special in the form. The first movement is a normal sonata form; the second is a kind of rondo with a development section in the middle. The last movement is difficult to define—mostly an augmented A-B-A form." Bartók's inversion of the traditional movement order creates an unorthodox framework for Quartet No. 2. The calm first movement is succeeded by a spirited allegro, and the slow finale projects an atmosphere of brooding melancholy. Bartók's friend Kodály observed that the quartet had an autobiographical basis and subtitled the work "Episodes: Peaceful life—Joy—Suffering."

The Moderato opens with a two-bar violin melody that provides the foundation for the entire movement. After its initial expansion, a three-note unit derived from an augmented triad and a tranquil third theme are developed with chromatic transitions. In the recapitulation, dissonant half-step intervals assume prominence. The closing section, with the theme heard in octaves in the first violin and viola accompanied by sliding parallel fifths in the cello, suggests the impressionist influence of Ravel. A coda combines the first and final themes, which can now be perceived as closely related.

Dominated by a barbaric ostinato, the Allegro evokes wild folk dance. Rapid changes from even to uneven meters build tension. The late Romantic harmonic background of the first movement has disappeared and is replaced by propelling percussive reiterations of dissonant intervals. A ghostly pall prevails at the pianissimo coda.

The primary theme of the plaintive Lento suggests a folk dirge. Its melodic outline is an actual quote of the main theme of the first movement, soon reduced to short sighing figures. The mode changes from major to minor, and rising thirds in the violins, steadily increasing in dynamic level, convey tragic weight. The work concludes in a subdued atmosphere with a cadence derived from Hungarian folksong.

String Quartet No. 3, Sz. 85

Prima parte: Moderato
Seconda parte: Allegro
Ricapitulazione della prima parte: Moderato
Coda: Allegro molto

The Third Quartet (1927) emerged after Bartók had closely explored the contrapuntal techniques of Bach and his predecessors. One hears passages of rigorous formal counterpoint as well as the continuous variation that is a leading characteristic of folk style. The briefest yet perhaps most intense of all Bartók's string quartets, the Third Quartet consists of one continuous flow of music divided into four sections to create a slow-fast-slow-fast format. The first and third sections are thematically related, as are the second and fourth. However, the connections between the first paired sections are not immediately obvious since section 3, the recapitulation, freely varies the motivic material.

The basic element of the Prima Parte is a three-note cell composed of two intervals—a rising fourth and a descending third. This motif is continuously developed so it is heard throughout the entire section. Especially remarkable is the area of "night music," subtle instrumental murmurs intended to evoke the rustling sounds of a mysterious forest.

The cello, playing pizzicato, introduces the pervasive motif of the rapid Seconda Parte—a simple scalar figure driven by a propulsive rhythm that evokes rural Hungarian dances. The section culminates with a dazzling fugue that further intensifies the rhythmic drive. Instrumental effects such as col legno (playing with the wood of the bow) and ponticello (bowing very near the bridge to achieve a glassy sound) contribute expressive color.

The "Recapitulation of the First Part" condenses and varies material heard in the first section, and its insistent three-note cell emerges strongly. The coda is essentially a transformation of the Seconda Parte with a denser contrapuntal texture. Percussive note repetitions, glissandi, and relentless ostinatos create a savage and aggressive character.

String Quartet No. 4, Sz. 91

Allegro
Prestissimo, con sordino
Non troppo lento
Allegretto pizzicato
Allegro molto

During the time Bartók wrote his Quartet No. 4, he was absorbed by the subtle and complex interrelationships heard in the late quartets of Beethoven. Structural allusions to these masterworks permeate Quartet No. 4, particularly in the outer movements. Bartók himself described Quartet No. 4 (1928): "The work is in five movements; their character corresponds to classical sonata form. The slow movement is the kernel of the work; the other movements are, as it were, arranged around it." Strong architectural symmetry is evident throughout Quartet No. 4. Two thematically connected movements (I and V) form the work's outer pillars. The substantial third movement, divided into three parts, falls at the work's center. This movement, the keystone, is framed by two thematically connected scherzo-like movements.

Vivid tone colors create a kaleidoscopic atmosphere throughout Quartet No. 4. Bartók introduces innovative instrumental techniques such as the "pizzicato glissando" (plucking the string while simultaneously sliding the finger) and the "Bartók pizzicato," in which the strings are pulled so strongly that they slap the fingerboard. Contrasts abound: several large sections are directed to be played with mutes to achieve a mysterious atmosphere, and other areas derive energy from "col legno," in which a passage is played sharply with the bow's wood.

The energetic Allegro, constructed in traditional sonata form, derives all its thematic content from a motif consisting of three rising and three falling notes, first heard in the cello. This material, continuously expanded and developed, returns in the fifth movement. The rapid second movement, muted throughout, departs significantly from traditional thematic structure. Rather than develop coherent melodic ideas, Bartók here explores fragmentary interval relationships, particularly the highly dissonant minor second.

The central movement opens with a cello solo based on a *táragató* melody—a slow moving, increasingly embellished line traditionally performed on an ancient Hungarian instrument related to the oboe. The middle section, the focal point of the entire quartet, contains what Bartók called "night music," evocations of bird calls and rustling forest sounds.

Bartók wrote about the fourth movement: "Its theme is the same as the main theme of the second movement. There it moves in the narrow intervals of the chromatic scale, but here it broadens in accordance with the diatonic style." All instruments play pizzicato throughout. Near its conclusion, the tumultuous finale quotes the first movement to unify the entire composition.

String Quartet No. 5, Sz. 102

Allegro
Adagio molto
Scherzo: Alla bulgarese
Andante
Finale: Allegro vivace

Quartet No. 5, dedicated to its commissioner Elizabeth Sprague Coolidge, was written with uncharacteristic speed during the month of August 1934. Its five movements are arranged symmetrically in an arch form. The first and fifth sections are rapid and share thematic material; the second and fourth are slow and similar in mood; a scherzo, with a central trio section, forms the center of the work. Mirror imaging can be discerned in the opening Allegro: at the recapitulation its three themes reappear inverted and in reverse order. The opening chorale theme of the Adagio molto suggests an homage to Beethoven's "Hymn of Thanksgiving" from his Opus 132 String Quartet; the following area of "night music," as in Quartet No. 4, is intended to evoke the murmur of a mysterious woods. Both ideas return with variations in the Andante fourth movement.

The central Scherzo moves in an irregular meter characteristic of Bulgarian folk song. Its measures, nine beats long, are divided so that accents fall at four, two, and three-beat units. The tempo accelerates in the trio section as the viola and cello sing a folklike melody.

The vitality of the opening Allegro returns in the presto finale, thematically based on the dissonant interval of the augmented fourth (B flat and E). A surprising shift occurs at the recapitulation—all dissonance disappears and the instruments are directed to play like a music box, "con indifferenza, meccanico" (with indifference, mechanically). Dissonance is gradually insinuated into the line and the vigorous Presto resumes.

String Quartet No. 6, Sz. 114

Mesto—Più mosso, pesante—Vivace
Mesto—Marcia
Mesto—Burletta: Moderato
Mesto

Possibly his most accessible quartet, Bartók's Quartet No. 6 exemplifies his so-called late classic period, in which he wrote with less dissonance, increased formal simplicity, and clearer themes. Written between August and November 1939, the quartet reflects Bartók's despair over the outbreak of World War II. The last work he composed in Hungary, the quartet premiered in 1941 after his emigration to the United States. The quartet's thematic content is based on a lament (*Mesto*, or mournful) that precedes each movement as a prologue. Different instruments—viola, cello, violin in turn—intone the lament, which grows in length and complexity in each movement. In the slow finale the lament becomes the central idea which all instruments share.

The primary motif of the first movement, inspired by Beethoven's late Opus 135 Quartet, resembles its famous theme set to the words *Muss es sein?* ("Must it be?"). A lively second theme suggests exuberant Hungarian folk dance. These two themes are developed and recapitulated in sonata form.

The body of the second movement is a march with strident dotted rhythmic patterns that conjure an atmosphere of anger and bitterness. Its central trio section is announced by a passionate cello solo accompanied by a violin tremolo and pizzicato in the viola. The opening march returns in a spectral guise.

Quartertone intervals between the two violins create a sardonic effect in the grotesque Burletta (farce), a dissonant movement relieved by its gentler trio section. The opening material returns with glissandi and aggressively percussive chords.

Themes heard in the first movement return in the finale but are now directed to be played "without warmth" and "far away." The final pizzicato notes of the cello suggest a somber farewell.

Contrasts for Clarinet, Violin, and Piano, Sz. 111

Verbunkos (Recruiting Dance)
Pihenő (Relaxation)
Sebes (Fast Dance)

Contrasts was conceptualized in 1938 at a convivial dinner enjoyed by Joseph Szigeti, the eminent Hungarian violinist, and Benny Goodman, the legendary jazz clarinetist. The two musicians decided to perform together, but they realized that their unique chemistry required new repertoire. The obvious choice of composer for their collaboration was Szigeti's compatriot Béla

Bartók, who could also perform with them as pianist during his projected 1940 visit to the U.S. Szigeti wrote to Bartók, who was then on vacation in Switzerland: "Benny has offered to triple the commission you usually receive. Please write him a registered letter, in which you agree to write a six to seven-minute clarinet and violin duo with piano accompaniment, the ownership of which remains yours. It would be very good if the composition were to consist of two independent sections which could be performed separately, and of course we hope it will include a brilliant clarinet and violin cadenza! Benny brings out whatever the clarinet is physically able to perform at all—in regions much higher than in *Eulenspiegel* (Richard Strauss's virtuoso tone poem)!" Within a month Bartók mailed the new work to its commissioners. He subsequently added a central movement and apologized that he now "delivered a suit for an adult instead of the dress ordered for a two-year-old baby."

Verbunkos depicts a vigorous recruiting dance traditionally performed by Hungarian army officers dressed in full regalia. This marchlike dance was most often accompanied by the *taragato*, a woodwind instrument popular for Hungarian folk music.

Pihenő, Hungarian for repose, was a late addition to the trio, which premiered as a two-movement work entitled *Rhapsody* in 1939. The expanded work was renamed *Contrasts* for its 1940 recording and Carnegie Hall performance with Bartók as pianist. Szegeti especially admired this slow interlude: "This 'night piece,' with its wonderful calm and free air, was highly necessary for balance."

For *Sebes*, or Fast Dance, the violinist must prepare a second violin tuned to the notes G sharp, D, A, and E flat in order to create the effect of a *danse macabre*. Its slower middle section is based on the asymmetrical Bulgarian dance rhythm of 3+2+3+2+3. The movement concludes with a violin cadenza and a virtuoso flourish from all three instruments.

FIFTEEN

Russian Modernity:
Shostakovich's Chamber Works

DMITRI SHOSTAKOVICH
B. SEPTEMBER 25, 1906 IN ST. PETERSBURG,
D. AUGUST 9, 1975 IN MOSCOW

STRING QUARTETS

The leading modernist Russian composer Dmitri Shostakovich began composition of his fifteen string quartets in 1936
and continued to write them throughout his creative life. Their
genesis was dramatic. Stalin had vehemently condemned and
banned Shostakovich's expressionist opera *Lady Macbeth of the
Mtsensk District* after a twenty-minute viewing because of its perceived amoral content and dissonance (the work was restored to
the repertory after Stalin's death). Out-of-favor artists most often
disappeared permanently during Stalin's dangerous regime, and
Shostakovich knew that to survive he had to regain favor with
the musically conservative Communist Party. He began to create
large-scale works with "official" messages embedded in them; but
he also began to write small-scale chamber works that could exist

below the Party radar. Since his impressive series of quartets—only one fewer than Beethoven, as Shostakovich was aware—began to emerge at this difficult time, they are often regarded as expressions of their composer's most private thoughts. Although this view is a simplification that minimizes the personal importance of his symphonies, it is undeniable that Shostakovich's most daring innovations of form and harmony are heard in his string quartets.

String Quartet No. 1 in C Major, Opus 49

Moderato
Moderato
Allegro molto
Allegro

After *Pravda* in 1936 denounced Shostakovich for "modernist formalism of the worst kind," he realized that more than just his career was at stake. Promising the authorities "a Soviet artist's practical creative reply to rightful criticism," Shostakovich revised his compositional style toward the harmonious and uplifting. He publicly wrote about his Quartet No. 1 (1938): "In composing my First Quartet, I visualized childhood scenes and somewhat naïve and bright moods associated with spring."

A pleasant work of overt simplicity, the quartet is written in a clear, transparent style. The work opens with a tranquil melody heard in the first violin; a songlike second theme is introduced by a glissando figure in the cello. After brief development, a varied restatement of themes concludes the movement. The Moderato offers three variations on a widely arcing theme that is remarkably both marchlike and soulful. The solo viola introduces the soaring melody, which suggests the character of Russian folk music. As the theme is developed by other instruments, it grows alternately fervent and pensive.

Shostakovich once claimed that the Allegro molto was his

favorite scherzo movement of all the quartets. Emotionally ambiguous, this rapid movement is played throughout with mutes to achieve the illusion of shadow; a lyrical central section varies the flow. The two themes of the joyous finale move through various changes of meter toward a virtuosic conclusion.

String Quartet No. 2 in A Major, Opus 68

Overture: Moderato con moto
Recitative and Romance: Adagio
Valse: Allegro
Theme and Variations

At the insistence of Soviet officials, Shostakovich in September 1944 relocated to Ovanovo, a government retreat for artists and writers a safe distance from war zones. Energized by his conviction that victory over Nazi Germany was imminent, Shostakovich wrote with white heat. Within three weeks he simultaneously produced his Quartet No. 2 and his substantial Piano Trio No. 2; both works were premiered together that November. Shostakovich wrote to his composer friend Shelbalin: "It is exactly twenty years since I first met you, and to commemorate the anniversary I would like to dedicate the quartet to you. I worry about the lightning speed with which I compose. Undoubtedly this is bad. It is exhausting, somewhat unpleasant, and at the end of the day you lack any confidence in the result. But I cannot rid myself of the bad habit." The most epic of his fifteen-quartet cycle, the work does not suggest overtly the duress of war; however, its quotations of Russian folk music illustrate his patriotism.

Shostakovich described the Overture as "a promise of things to come." This theatrical and quasi-symphonic movement (A major) develops two spirited ideas in sonata form. The mood becomes ambiguous as the tonality shifts to minor, but the movement concludes with jubilance in the major key.

The second movement, Recitative and Romance (B flat major), opens with an extended violin cantilena accompanied by simple chords in the other instruments. Initially a pensive statement, the Romance develops with fervor as other voices join. The violin soliloquy returns to suggest a lone voice in the crowd—perhaps a reminder that individuals exist within the immense collective event of the war.

Shostakovich states that the darkly-keyed third movement (E flat minor) "is a *valse macabre*. And if it were to be compared to the classics, it should be compared to the Waltz from the Third Suite by Tchaikovsky." Played with mutes throughout, this rapid and sinister movement is based on the second subject of the first movement.

As a connection to the waltz, the finale opens with a brief adagio section in E flat minor. The ensuing variations movement (A minor) is based on the Russian folk theme also heard in his Piano Trio No. 2. Its thirteen variations begin in a tranquil atmosphere, but their mood gradually grows intense and fervent. After an agitated climax, the calm mood returns with a chorale-like section in B major. A reflective reprise leads to a clear statement of the theme in the first violin. An Adagio section (A minor) brings the work to a powerful conclusion.

String Quartet No. 3 in F Major, Opus 73

Allegretto
Moderato con moto
Allegro non troppo
Adagio
Moderato—Adagio

Guided by the musical preferences of Joseph Stalin, Soviet authorities urged composers to create heroic works that drew from folk tradition. Shostakovich indicated that his projected Symphony

No. 9 (1945) would offer the desired uplifting statement. However, at its premiere the symphony was heard as mere entertainment, and Shostakovich was denounced for "formalism"—defined by the Soviets as "elitist catering to purely individual experiences of a small clique of aesthetes while rejecting the classical heritage." Shostakovich did not undertake another symphony until Stalin's death in 1953; more private composition of his quartet series offered a refuge. Soon after the debacle of his Ninth Symphony, Shostakovich began his Quartet No. 3.

Shostakovich originally conceived his Opus 73 (1946) as a war statement, and he created programmatic subtitles for its five movements:

I.   Calm awareness of the future cataclysm
II. Rumblings of unrest and anticipation
III. The forces of war unleashed
IV. Homage to the dead
V.   The eternal question: Why? And for what?

Shostakovich suppressed these subtitles, but many groups such as the Borodin Quartet insist on their inclusion whenever they perform the work.

The musical progression of Opus 73 generally follows the emotional affect of its subtitles. The sonata form Movement I begins in a lighthearted atmosphere, but ever more frenzied development (a double fugue with fast-moving harmonies) and a final acceleration of tempo conjures agitation.

Movement II is a sardonic waltz. Passagework grows lugubrious near the end as the instruments descend into their lower registers.

Movement III (F minor), perhaps an echo of the sinister Scherzo movement from Symphony No. 5, is a ferocious and martial statement. Its two themes, heard in the violin and cello, are accompanied by strident chords in the other instruments. The movement ends abruptly.

Movement IV is a passacaglia (a stately seventeenth-century form built on a repeating bass line) that opens with all instruments in unison. A violin soliloquy leads to a somber cello lament, accompanied by pizzicati in the viola; the viola assumes the lament, now accompanied by cello pizzicati. After fugal development, the movement ends quietly.

Movement V opens with a jaunty cello theme that recalls the opening of the quartet. As the tempo grows faster, the atmosphere becomes anguished. Sustained notes in the solo cello halt the momentum. The violin plays a poignant theme that is possibly of Jewish origin. The violin plays ever higher as it poses its question: Why? What is it for?

String Quartet No. 4 in D Major, Opus 83

Allegretto
Andantino
Allegretto
Allegretto

Shostakovich reached artistic maturity at the midpoint of the century, a time when USSR intellectual and cultural stagnation was so extreme that reportedly even the Stalinist authorities who created it were uncomfortable with what they had wrought. Especially between the years 1946 and 1952 it was customary for Shostakovich to premiere works assured of state approval, such as the 1952 cantata *Song of the Motherland*, but to hide potentially controversial works in his bottom drawer and hope for better times. One such protected work was his Quartet No. 4, written in 1949 but premiered in 1953 after Stalin's death. This quartet risked censure because of its Jewish themes, politically unpopular among the Stalinists. Shostakovich, who composed several works based on Jewish material during these years, wrote: "By setting these themes I might be able to tell the fate of the Jewish people. It is an important thing to do because I can see anti-Semitism growing all around me." The work is now one of the most frequently performed of Shostakovich's quartets in Russia.

Quartet No. 4 opens in a popular atmosphere as the violins play folklike themes of Jewish origin while the viola and cello imitate a hurdy-gurdy with sustained pedal notes. Emerging dissonances gradually create pandemonium, but the movement ends quietly with a return of the violin theme over supporting pedal tones. The lyrical Andantino is an unorthodox waltz that alternates between triple and duple meter. The quartet's emotional center, this F minor movement develops with a variety of affecting harmonies.

The Allegretto, muted throughout, is a scherzo that develops with subtle instrumental colors. A recurring dotted rhythmic figure underpins the melodic material, which echoes the Jewish themes of the opening movement. The richly inventive finale, full of colorful pizzicati and glissandi, often suggests a grotesque dance. After an impassioned section that moves through various meters, the gentler mood of the Andantino returns. The movement ends quietly with hushed pizzicati under a sustained high note in the cello.

String Quartet No. 5 in B flat Major, Opus 92

Allegro non troppo
Andante—Andantino—Andante—Andantino—Andante
Moderato—Allegretto—Andante

Shostakovich wrote his Quartet No. 5 in the fall of 1952 and dedicated the work to the Beethoven Quartet, who premiered the work the following November. Because Shostakovich suspected that Stalin would have reacted negatively to Opus 92 because of its personal content, it was premiered only after his death. Its three movements are performed without pause, a new formal development for Shostakovich and one that he would continue in subsequent works. The quartet reveals the composer's fluent counterpoint, a favorite technique that he developed further after he had participated as judge for J.S. Bach's 1950 bicentenary competitions in Leipzig. Shortly before composing his Quartet No. 5, Shostakovich wrote his 24 Preludes and Fugues for Piano as homage to Bach.

Two highly personal motifs organize the quartet. The primary motif is based on the musical spelling of his signature DSCH (D-E flat-C-B), with S corresponding to the note E flat and H the German equivalent to the note B. (This motif is heard as permutations in the following three quartets and becomes structurally significant in Quartet No. 8.) The viola introduces this motif at the beginning of the Allegro non troppo. The second personal motif consists of several bars quoted from the Clarinet Trio in B flat Major written by his student, Galina Ustvolskaya. Following the recent death of his first wife, Shostakovich had proposed marriage to Galina, but to his acute disappointment she refused him. Agitated counterpoint between these two personal themes creates an atmosphere of frenzied longing. The closing section grows calmer as Galina's theme is played by the first violin and Shostakovich's motif follows in the viola. The first violin plays a sustained high F, which leads directly into the next movement.

The second movement quotes themes from earlier Shostakovich works that had remained unpublished until Stalin's death. Ideas from the second and final movements of Quartet No. 3, as well as his violin concerto, are developed with spare, sustained lines that conjure deep stillness.

The finale opens in a sanguine atmosphere (Moderato), but the agitated mood of the opening movement returns (Allegretto). The tempo slows at the Andante section, and the violin plays a reflective soliloquy that suggests the austerity of the second movement. The cello assumes the melody, which becomes a nostalgic waltz that conjures the old Europe. An extended cello reverie follows, then a violin statement accompanied by sustained chords.

The movement concludes on a quiet B flat major chord with the directive "morendo" (dying).

String Quartet No. 6 in G Major, Opus 101

Allegretto
Moderato con moto
Lento
Lento—Allegretto—Andante—Lento

In the summer of 1956 Shostakovich, then a widower with two children, decided to remarry. The attractive Margarita Kainova caught his eye, and to contrive an introduction he purchased a pair of opera tickets and sent her one anonymously. However, Margarita was not a music lover, and she gave away the ticket. Arriving at the opera he was distressed to discover her seat occupied by a stranger. Undaunted, he then asked a colleague to set up a meeting. The shy composer shocked friends and family by proposing to Margarita that same afternoon. Shostakovich explained: "She is a good woman, and I hope she will be a good wife to me and a good mother for my children." However, he should have realized when the opera ticket stratagem failed that he had little in common with Margarita, and after three years Shostakovich filed for divorce. But that first August Shostakovich was a relaxed man on his honeymoon, during which he undertook composition of his Quartet No. 6 in G Major, Opus 101. He completed the quartet within days and reported that for the first time in years he was satisfied with a new work. Although Opus 101 cannot be described as one of the composer's grander quartets, its genial affect attests to the range and diversity of Shostakovich's formidable contribution to the genre.

The harmonies of Quartet No. 6 are basically diatonic. However, before each movement reaches its final cadence, it articulates the pungent chord D-E flat-C-B—a musical spelling of DSCH,

Shostakovich's characteristic signature. The carefree opening Allegretto leads into the dancelike Moderato movement (E flat major), which is varied by a chromatic section at its center. The reflective Lento (B flat minor) is a passacaglia, a set of eloquent variations over a ten-bar theme intoned by the cello. The complex finale, in sonata-rondo form, proceeds without pause. As its two themes build to an exuberant peak, themes from the earlier movements are recalled, now varied in tempo. The movement ends quietly with all instruments muted.

String Quartet No. 7 in F sharp Minor, Opus 108

Allegretto
Lento
Allegro—Allegretto

Shostakovich's Quartet No. 7 (1960) is a birthday remembrance for his adored first wife, Nina Varzar, who had died six years earlier but would have celebrated her fiftieth had she lived. Critics consider Opus 108 to be the first of his final group of quartets, works through which he sought to offer thoughts on life, death, and immortality. Many listeners have attributed the increasingly melancholy atmosphere in these later works to Nina's early death.

Written with the utmost economy of texture, Quartet No. 7 develops its ideas primarily through extended solo, duo, or trio passages rather than full quartet voicing. This deliberate sparseness especially enhances the sense of desolation in the austere central movement (Lento), the cool heart of the quartet. The opening Allegretto explores two chromatic themes made whimsical by frequent meter changes. At its recapitulation the first theme, played pizzicato in triple meter, is transformed into a bizarre waltz, which reappears in the closing section of the finale.

After a brief introduction, played with mutes in all instruments, the Allegro finale restates the chromatic viola motif heard at the end of the Lento and develops it as a spectral waltz. The movement concludes with a quiet coda.

String Quartet No. 8 in C Minor, Opus 110

Largo
Allegro molto
Allegretto
Largo
Largo

In the summer of 1960 Shostakovich travelled to Dresden to compose the score for a commemorative war film entitled "Five Days, Five Nights." Surrounded by evidence of this once glorious city's destruction, Shostakovich recalled his own horrific experiences during the Siege of Leningrad. While intensely focused on these vivid memories, Shostakovich created his eighth string quartet, an autobiographical statement in music written feverishly within the period of three days. Dedicated "in memory of victims of fascism and war," the quartet develops with a fervor that sets it among the most compelling of Shostakovich's fifteen string quartets.

To suggest his reliving of memories from the siege of Leningrad, Opus 110 includes substantial quotations from works that Shostakovich had created during the war's duration. The recurring motto heard throughout the quartet consists of the musical spelling of Shostakovich's own name—the notes D-E flat-C-B represent the initials "D.Sch" (Sch being the German transliteration of the single Russian character that begins his surname).

The five movements of the quartet are performed without pause. The cello introduces the composer's personal motto in the opening Largo, formally a rondo that includes quotations from Shostakovich's first and fifth symphonies. Shostakovich portrays the war's brutality most vividly in the frenzied second movement, which evokes the relentless bombing of Dresden. A quotation of the "Jewish theme" heard in the second piano trio recalls the horrific discovery of the death camps, here specifically the one at Majdanek, one of the first to be liberated by the Red Army. The third movement, a sardonic waltz, includes a fragment of the first cello concerto, which recurs as a motif for the fourth movement. The Largo's second theme, based on the Russian revolutionary song *Languishing in Prison*, is intoned by the three lower instruments. At the Largo's climax the cello sings an aria from Shostakovich's opera *Lady Macbeth of the Mtsensk District*, which Stalin condemned in 1936. The final Largo, which recalls the opening movement, is a slow fugato based on the motif DSCH. Shostakovich intended for this movement to live as an epitaph for all who fell in the fight against Nazism.

String Quartet No. 9 in E flat Major, Opus 117

Moderato con moto
Adagio
Allegretto
Adagio
Allegro

Shostakovich completed his austere and dramatic ninth quartet during the summer of 1964, four years after he had written his powerful Quartet No. 8. An earlier version of Quartet No. 9, based on favorite themes from his childhood, was discarded. He wrote: "In an attack of self-criticism I burned it in the stove. This is the second such case in my creative practice. The new quartet is completely different."

The quartet's five movements contain no literary program but reveal numerous personal motifs—such as his musical signature DSCH, played as D-E flat-C-B natural. Unified by common thematic and textural elements, the movements are performed without pause. The varied emotional range of Quartet No. 9—conveyed through biting sforzandi, glissandi, and passages of eerily thin texture that suggest the border of consciousness—anticipates Shostakovich's late style.

The opening Moderato (E flat major), written in classical sonata form, develops three subjects that recur in the final movements. The poignant Adagio that follows (F sharp minor) is an emotional dialogue between the first violin and viola. The Allegretto third movement (F sharp minor alternating with the major) is a three-part scherzo with a songful middle section contrasting with dissonant and menacing outer sections. The stark Adagio fourth movement (E flat minor-major) explores two alternating themes that were foreshadowed in the earlier movements. The Allegro finale, cast in five sections, at moments evokes a wild central Asian folk dance that Shostakovich heard while visiting Tashkent shortly before he began writing the quartet's second version. Its development section, which begins softly and gradually reaches fortissimo, culminates in a brilliant fugue built on variants of the principal subject. The intense closing section builds contrapuntally to a forceful climax as themes from previous movements are recapitulated.

String Quartet No. 10 in A flat Major, Opus 118

Andante
Allegretto furioso
Adagio
Allegretto—Andante

The appealing Quartet No. 10 was written during the spring and summer of 1964 for Shostakovich's friend, the prolific but little-known composer Moishe Vainberg (aka Mieczysław Weinberg). With the exception of the densely scored second movement (Allegretto furioso) the quartet develops with forms and textures simpler than his earlier quartets. This lyrical work has become one of Shostakovich's most popular chamber compositions.

The solo violin introduces the gentle thematic material of the opening Andante, and the other instruments respond with a passage of restrained three-part polyphony. The material is recapitulated in a muted ponticello passage (instruments played "at the bridge" to produce a glassy sound).

A scherzo with relentless fortissimo dynamics, the Allegretto furioso (E minor) is a strident contrast to the opening movement. The first violin introduces the aggressive main theme, and the cello articulates the agitated second theme in its upper register. A variation of the opening idea returns as a violin duet. Because of its savagely dissonant harmonies, demanding octave lines in the violins, and rapid accents, this movement requires the utmost stamina and virtuosity.

The ethereal Adagio is cast as a strict passacaglia, a baroque form in which variations are built over a repeated "ground" in the bass line. Heard primarily in the cello, this ground pattern recurs nine times as the other instruments explore the theme, which is richly harmonized and ornamented with countermelodies. The movement closes with a suspended A flat major chord as the viola initiates the finale, which proceeds without pause.

The Allegretto resembles a wild Russian *trepak*, a dance of the Steppes. Its opening two subjects are heard initially in the viola: the first theme, animated by a repeating rhythmic figure, revolves around a single note, and the second idea reiterates a simple motif against a continuous drone in the other instruments. A transformation of the second movement's scherzo theme accompanied by pizzicati creates a contrasting new idea. A long crescendo leads to a restatement of the Adagio's passacaglia theme in the cello; the momentum slows as themes from earlier movements return. At the Andante section the first movement's opening theme, now heard in the cello, returns in a slower tempo. The work concludes in the calm spirit of its opening.

String Quartet No. 11 in F Minor, Opus 122

Introduction: Andantino
Scherzo: Allegretto
Recitative: Adagio
Etude: Allegro
Humoresque: Allegro
Elegy: Adagio
Finale: Moderato

Quartet No. 11 is a memorial tribute to Vasily Petrovich Shirinsky, longtime second violinist with the Beethoven Quartet—the premiering group for the majority of Shostakovich's string quartets. Ostensibly the celebration of a musical life, Quartet No. 11 develops with the spare texture and lean harmonies often heard in his late quartets. Alan George, violist with the Shostakovich Quartet and an esteemed colleague of the composer, describes the work: "The Quartet inhabits a strangely withdrawn region which in the end is deeply touching. The casting of the work into seven highly contrasting movements, rather like a suite of character pieces, might seem to have run a risk of diffuseness; but at this stage of his career Shostakovich was firmly committed to continuity and cogency in his quartets. He achieves a disarmingly simple unity through stringent economy of means; the work is constructed on only two motifs, both subjected to Shostakovich's highly developed technique for exploiting all latent possibilities. So all the characters are in reality the same one: the same clown with different faces, be it tender, whimsical, severe, mercurial, droll, elegiac, or the simple 'yurodivy' (the traditional Russian 'Holy Fool').

"Up to the end of the fourth movement all the violin solos have been taken by the first violin. The irony is that the quartet is dedicated to the memory of a second violinist. But he can play only two notes, and he manages to keep them up throughout the entire Humoresque—which doesn't even get its own tempo, there being no change of pulse from the preceding Etude. All this represents a wry comment on the role of the second violin and also reflects Shirinsky's droll sense of humor.

"Eventually we come to the real purpose of this piece: an elegy that begins with great seriousness and intensity. Its dominant rhythm perhaps recalls the *Eroica* Symphony for the Beethoven Quartet, and is grimly prophetic of the Funeral March in Quartet No. 15—composed after the death of Shirinsky's brother, the cellist in the quartet."

String Quartet No. 12 in D flat Major, Opus 133

Moderato—Allegretto
Allegretto—Adagio—Moderato—Allegretto

As appreciation for his long association with the Beethoven Quartet Shostakovich dedicated string quartets to each of its current members. With Quartet No. 12 (1968) he honored first violinist Dmitri Tsyganov, a player known for his darkly expressive "Russian" sound, and also extended his previous quartet's tribute to the recently deceased second violinist Vasily Shirinsky. Shostakovich wrote Quartet No. 12 in a self-described "non-conformist" two movement format. The composer himself provided a brief explanation: "The first movement portrays the world of high ideals. The second movement stands in sharp contrast to it. Its first (as well as third) section presents a disturbing 'Scherzo,' an agony, which is unable to cope with the contradictions of life."

The opening Moderato sets up a harmonic duality between modernist atonality and traditional tonality. Introduced by the solo cello, the work opens atonally with a twelve-tone row as pioneered by Schoenberg—all notes of the chromatic scale arranged in a specific sequence without repeats. This unsettled statement leads to a singing passage in a clear D flat major tonality. The ensuing sections are connected by recurrences of the twelve-note row in the solo instruments.

Always aware of the significance of numbers, Shostakovich contrives an extra-musical statement by delaying the entrance of the second violin until measure 34. The Beethoven Quartet had played for 34 years with violinist Vasily Shirinsky, who had recently died. As a tribute, the new violinist must wait that many measures before sounding his voice.

Movement II combines elements of traditional scherzo, adagio, and finale movement forms into one continuous section. Its rapid, atonal opening area ends with an extended mysterious passage played ponticello (on the bridge). This section has been described as one of the most unusual and sinister passages in all of Shostakovich's quartets. The Adagio that follows consists of an extended cello solo accompanied by chords in the other instruments. The movement closes with a dramatic synthesis of the themes that have been developed throughout the work.

String Quartet No. 13 in B flat Minor, Opus 138

Adagio—Doppio movimento—Tempo primo

Quartet No. 13 (1970) was described by *Pravda* following its premiere: "It is a meditation upon the brevity of man's life, and a passionate glorification of the beauty and majesty of the human spirit which asserts itself despite the inexorable fatefulness of nature."

Shostakovich dedicated the quartet to Vadim Borisovsky, a founding member of the Beethoven Quartet and its violist for 40 years. The viola line is prominent throughout the quartet, and its technical and expressive possibilities are explored to a degree rare in chamber literature. Quartet No. 13 is written in the form of three extended sections played without pause. The unaccompanied viola introduces the Adagio's elegiac opening theme, constructed on the twelve notes of the chromatic scale, and concludes the movement with a high solo recitative. Three strongly dissonant chords lead to the Doppio movimento section, which moves at twice the speed of the opening Adagio. A quasi scherzo with an aura of fantasy, the section opens with a sinister idea in the first violin as the other instruments accompany with percussive bow clacks on the wood of their instruments. In the mysterious final Tempo primo section the opening Adagio idea returns as the viola and cello engage in a solemn dialogue. The viola reprises the main ideas with an extended solo, accompanied by percussive bow tapping. The viola song resumes, rises, and abruptly ends.

String Quartet No. 14 in F sharp Minor, Opus 142

Allegretto
Adagio
Allegretto—Adagio

When Shostakovich's health began to deteriorate near the end of his life, he attempted to summarize his thoughts on life, death, and immortality through his chamber works. Among other conditions, he suffered nerve impairment of his right hand, a possible reason for the leaner scoring in these late quartets.

Shostakovich began Quartet No. 14 while he was visiting Benjamin Britten at his home in England in 1972. Shostakovich's violinist colleague Christopher Rowland conveyed the composer's ideas about the quartet in an interview: "The existence of a fourteenth quartet was casually mentioned in a letter written to me from Copenhagen on May 4, 1973. The following March the music arrived with a covering letter apologizing for the delay and explaining that he had been very ill and therefore unable to write it out.

"Because of its spare texture, it is very easy to underestimate the Fourteenth Quartet. Yet few people underestimate Mahler's Tenth Symphony, despite its incompleteness, and the two works say strikingly similar things to us—as well as being rooted in the same key, F sharp minor. These two works leave us in similar emotional states—a recognition of a painful longing for life which is slipping away, and a passionate love and desire to be alive. The Fourteenth Quartet shares with the other late works an atmosphere of private contemplation—yet this quartet is unique because of its impassioned radiance."

The Allegretto opens with a viola statement that introduces the lyrical main idea, treated fugally by the first violin and cello. This delicate theme combines with chromatic interludes to create a poignant atmosphere. The emotional center of the work is the sparely written Adagio (D minor), which offers soliloquies between the first violin and the cello-—homage to the quartet's dedicatee, cellist Sergei Shirinsky. The impetuous Allegretto finale (F sharp minor) alludes thematically to the earlier movements; the mood grows serene at its Adagio conclusion.

String Quartet No. 15 in E flat Minor, Opus 144

Elegy: Adagio
Serenade: Adagio
Intermezzo: Adagio
Nocturne: Adagio
Funeral March: Adagio molto
Epilogue

The year before his death from heart disease Shostakovich wrote his final string quartet. Many listeners have heard this work as his own requiem. Quartet No. 15 (1974) consists of six profoundly moving adagios, played without pause. The work opens with a quiet fugal lament, an elegy that recalls the Russian Orthodox style. In the second movement each instrument in turn articulates a poignant cry through a single sustained note that begins in a soft dynamic but grows ever stronger. The following Serenade conjures a macabre atmosphere; it ends with a pianissimo pedal note in the cello that leads into the brief but furious Intermezzo. The Nocturne moves with undulating figuration in the second violin and cello that underpins a plaintive melody sung by the viola. Near its conclusion an ominous pizzicato figure in the violins foreshadows the Funeral March, emphatically announced by all instruments in unison. Solo passages for the first violin, viola, and cello form the basis of the movement; the march is interjected as a refrain. The spectral finale quotes themes from the earlier movements before it concludes quietly with a somber chant.

Shostakovich had intended to write sixteen string quartets to equal Beethoven's oeuvre. Although his death deprived him from reaching that goal, the fifteen quartets that exist are the gems of the modern Russian repertory.

WORKS WITH VARIED SCORING

Piano Trio No. 2 in E Minor, Opus 67

Andante—Moderato
Allegro con brio
Largo
Allegretto

In September 1944 Shostakovich wrote his second piano trio as a tribute to his recently deceased friend, the musicologist Ivan Sollertinsky. Earlier that year, Sollertinsky, although a young man, had died of a heart attack incurred while evacuating the war zone in Leningrad. Shostakovich described his jovial and eccentric friend: "He was a brilliant scholar who spoke dozens of languages and kept his diary in ancient Portuguese to keep it safe from prying eyes.

He found great pleasure in a merry and liberated life, even though he worked very hard. Sadly, people will probably only remember that his tie was askew and that a new suit on him looked old in five minutes."

Sollertinsky introduced Shostakovich to music of the eastern European Jews, and it affected him profoundly. He stated: "This music can appear to be happy when it is tragic. It is multi-faceted ... laughter through tears." Throughout his memorial trio, Shostakovich incorporates themes suggestive of both Russian folk song and ethnic Jewish dance music. At the time he composed the trio, Shostakovich had just received grim reports about the massacres of Jewish concentration camp inmates at the hands of the Nazis. Although he never professed programmatic intentions, many listeners at the work's premiere heard depictions of doomed persons dancing at the edges of their graves in the work's finale.

The elegiac Andante begins with a remarkable sonority—a wistful theme played in high harmonics by the cello accompanied by the violin in its lowest register. After this introduction, the movement develops folklike themes in a calm atmosphere. The following scherzo movement, propelled by energetic dance rhythms, conveys turbulent joie de vivre.

The Largo is a dark and funereal chaconne built on repetitions of eight chords intoned by the piano as the violin and cello sing a continuously varied, sorrowful duet. This powerful movement serves as the introduction to the finale, the dramatic center of the trio. Tension builds as ever more frenzied themes suggest macabre dances of death. Fragments of the earlier themes return. The closing notes, a quiet recollection of the movement's beginning, suggest serene resolution.

Piano Quintet in G Minor, Opus 57

Prelude: Lento—Poco più mosso—Lento
Fugue: Adagio
Scherzo: Allegretto
Intermezzo: Lento
Finale: Allegretto

Shostakovich created his Opus 57 Piano Quintet in 1940, a year of calm between storms in Soviet Russia. The Great Terror, during which hundreds of artists and writers were arrested and often killed, had mostly subsided, and Germany did not yet threaten to invade. Shostakovich realized that he was fortunate to be able to write. Stalin, the author of the Terror, had viewed Shostakovich with suspicion ever since he angrily left a 1936 performance of the composer's expressionist opera *Lady Macbeth of the Mtsensk District*. Soon after, both Stalin and *Pravda* vehemently denounced Shostakovich for writing decadent music that lacked correct moral and social values. The composer's career was temporarily stalled.

Stalin considered Beethoven to be the first "Social realist" composer and insisted on an esthetic not far removed from eighteenth-century tradition. Despite this constraint, Shostakovich achieved personal expression by channeling his private thoughts through the intimate medium of chamber music. To insure survival he earned party favor by producing deliberately simple, conventional, and grand works that celebrated various Soviet endeavors such as Stalin's reforestation plan. It is a measure of Shostakovich's successful musical diplomacy that when the Nazis invaded Leningrad in 1941, Stalin insisted that Shostakovich be airlifted to the relative safety of eastern Russia. Doubtless this was a dubious honor for the patriotic Shostakovich, who only three months earlier had placed himself in danger to defend Muscovites from enemy bombs.

Stalin admired the Opus 57 Piano Quintet and awarded it the 1940 "Stalin Prize." This immense cash award of 100,000 rubles was perhaps justified by the enthusiastic public response—at its premiere the ensemble repeated the Scherzo and Finale to satisfy the cheering crowd. However, Western critics were skeptical of a work so strongly endorsed by the Soviet government. Despite its conservative formal structure, the Quintet did eventually win wide critical acceptance because of its fine themes and superb craftsmanship.

Shostakovich wrote his Opus 57 at the request of the Soviet Union's Beethoven Quartet, which had asked him to perform as their pianist. Prominent throughout the Quintet, the piano introduces and develops many of the work's thematic ideas. The contemplative three-part Prelude leads without pause to the Fugue, influenced by J.S. Bach. Scored initially for strings, this contrapuntal movement opens with a somber theme that suggests Russian folk origin. Momentum gradually builds to an impassioned thematic statement then slowly subsides to a hush.

Brilliantly colorful string effects—glissandos, pizzicatos, upper register passages—give vibrancy to the explosive Scherzo. This hard-driving movement careens to a stunning conclusion.

The broadly melodic Intermezzo opens with a lyrical passage in the first violin; drama increases as other instruments enter. The rhapsodic finale follows without pause. The piano introduces its two themes, first a subdued motif then an angular second idea, famed as the clowns' entrance music in the Russian circus. The work concludes quietly with a gentle statement derived from the movement's first theme.

Useful Terms

Adagio: A very slow and leisurely tempo.

Allegro: A fast and lively tempo.

Andante: A moderately slow tempo.

Andantino: Slightly faster than Andante, of which it is the diminutive.

Aria: In instrumental music an extended songful passage most often scored for one instrument.

Arpeggio: The consecutive articulation of ascending or descending chord tones.

Atonality: Broadly defined as "without a key center," this term emerged in the early twentieth century as composers explored schemes that diverged from the prevailing diatonic (strongly tonal) harmony based on major and minor Western scale patterns.

Cadenza: A virtuoso, often improvised solo passage derived from earlier thematic material. A cadenza is most often heard near the end of a movement.

Cantilena: A lyrical melodic passage.

Chromatic: Literally "colorful," chromatic notes are half-step inserts between notes of the major or minor scale.

Col legno: The player strikes the instrument "with the wood" of the bow.

Con brio: With spirit.

Con moto: With motion. Often used as a modification for a tempo marking (e.g., Allegro con moto).

Consonance: A harmonious combination of notes.

Counterpoint: Two or more themes woven together, either as points of imitation with each other or paired as a theme and complementary countertheme.

Cyclic form: Significant thematic material recurs throughout a work for structural unification.

Diatonic scale: The seven notes of the major or minor scale; the seven diatonic triads constructed from these constitute the basis of much Western music.

Dissonance: A combination of notes heard as discord.

Exposition: See "Sonata form."

Expressionism: A modernist movement originating in German visual arts that conveys heightened emotional experience, most often through atonality.

Figured bass: A Baroque notation system in which an accompaniment is improvised from a bass line provided with numerals indicating the desired harmonies.

Forte (Italian "strong"): A loud dynamic.

Fugue: Imitative counterpoint in which one instrument passes a theme on to succeeding instruments; counterthemes and devices such as rhythmic augmentation (lengthening of note values) and thematic inversion (the subject appears upside down) can introduce complexity.

Glissando: A continuous tone produced by sliding from one pitch to another.

Impressionism: Influenced by French symbolist literature and painting, this style conjures atmosphere through colorfully nuanced harmonies, scorings, and subtle shifts of rhythm.

Largo (Italian "broad"): A stately tempo, slower than Adagio.

Minuet (or Italian, Menuetto): A triple-time movement of French dance origin that often appears centrally in a multi-movement work. A trio section contrasting in theme and often reduced in scoring occurs between the two repetitions of the opening material.

Motif (or motive): A brief musical idea.

Mute: A mechanical device used to soften instrumental sound and alter tone color by reducing vibrations.

Non troppo (Italian "not too much"; sometimes ma non troppo, "but not too much"): A tempo modification, i.e., Allegro non troppo.

Octet: A composition for eight instruments.

Ostinato: An extended repetition of a specific note group.

Piano (Italian "soft"): A quiet dynamic marking.

Piano Quartet: An ensemble comprised of a violin, viola, cello, and piano.

Piano Quintet: An ensemble comprised of two violins, viola, cello, and piano.

Piano Trio: An ensemble consisting of a violin, cello, and piano, perhaps the most popular combination in chamber music after the string quartet.

Pizzicato: The string is plucked with the finger to achieve a short, emphatic sound.

Ponticello: The bow is drawn very near the bridge to emphasize the higher overtones and achieve a glassy sound.

Presto (Italian "quickly"): A very rapid tempo.

Quintet: A composition for five instruments.

Recapitulation: See "Sonata form."

Recitative: A rhythmically free style that imitates speech.

Rondo: Most often heard as a final movement, the form is structured as A-B-A-C-A, with A as the main theme, the B and C sections as contrasting interludes.

Scherzo: A playful, triple-time central movement, often faster than its predecessor, the minuet. A brief trio section, so called because it was originally scored for three players, alternates with repetitions of the opening material.

Septet: A composition for seven instruments.

Sextet: A composition for six instruments.

Sonata form: The prevailing structure for the majority of first movements in the Classic and Romantic eras. There are three essential parts. First, the exposition introduces the various themes, which are most often of a complementary character; the entire section is customarily repeated. Second, the development manipulates the stated themes in a variety of ways—recasting them with new harmonies, recombining components of a theme with new material, or expanding thematic elements to create a related statement that is essentially heard as new. The third component is the recapitulation, a section of restatement; the original tonalities and themes of the exposition return, most often with alterations that enhance but do not change their character. The entire movement may be prefaced with an introduction and concluded with a coda. Sonata form opening movements are generally followed by a slow movement (most often in song form, see below), a minuet, and a rapid finale.

Song form: Borrowed from vocal music, this A-B-A instrumental form is often heard in slow movements. The central section frequently varies ideas introduced in the opening A section.

Staccato: The note is quickly articulated with separation from the note following.

String Quartet: An ensemble consisting of two violins, viola, and cello. It became popular beginning in the latter part of the eighteenth century and remains the dominant genre of chamber music.

String Trio: An ensemble usually comprised of violin, viola, and cello.

Syncopation: An expected accent is shifted to an unexpected beat within the measure.

Tremolo (Italian "trembling"): The bow moves rapidly back and forth on the same note.

Trill: A note alternates rapidly with the note above.

Variation form: A theme is transformed rhythmically, melodically, or harmonically to reveal its different guises.

Sources

Primary Sources

Recordings and (ideally) scores are the starting points for the appreciation of chamber music. Public libraries often own selections of both, and university libraries are incomparable. YouTube is a personal favorite resource. Many of the compositions play concurrently with their companion score, and one can easily compare different interpretations, all listed with their performance times (which can vary significantly). Other streaming media resources are also excellent. Needless to say, concert attendance is invaluable!

Composers' commentaries on their music can be found in both their collected letters (e.g., Brahms, *Letters*) and selected volumes of composer readings: *The Mozart Compendium, The Beethoven Reader, The Schubert Reader, A Brahms Reader*. Autobiographies (e.g., Shostakovich, *Testimony*) began to emerge during the literary-minded Romantic era. Reliable biographical studies that include substantial quotations from the composers also are important sources (e.g., R. Larry Todd, *Mendelssohn: A Life in Music*).

PUBLICATIONS WITH COMMENTARY FROM COMPOSERS AND THEIR COLLEAGUES

Avins, Styra, ed. *Johannes Brahms: Letters*. Oxford University Press, 1997.

Arnold, Denis, and Nigel Fortune, eds. *The Beethoven Reader*. Norton, 1971.

Deutsch, Otto Erich. *Mozart: A Documentary Biography*. Stanford University Press, 1965.

Deutsch, Otto Erich. *The Schubert Reader: A Life of Franz Schubert in Letters and Documents*. Norton, 1963.

Landon, H. C. Robbins, *The Mozart Compendium*. Thames and Hudson, 1996.

Musgrave, Michael. *A Brahms Reader*. Yale University Press, 2000.

Volkov, Solomon, ed. *Testimony: The Memoirs of Dmitri Shostakovich*. Harper and Row, 1979.

Secondary Sources: A Selected Bibliography

Both the signed articles in the *The New Grove Dictionary of Music and Musicians* and the individually published books from their composers' series are fine starting points because of their thorough coverage and excellent bibliographies.

Carpenter, Humphrey. *Benjamin Britten: A Biography*. Harper and Row, 1979.

Chalmers, Kenneth. *Béla Bartók*. Phaidon, 1995.

Clapham, John. *Dvořák*. Trafalgar Square, 1991.

Einstein, Alfred. *Schubert: A Musical Portrait*. Oxford University Press, 1951.

Jensen, Eric Frederick. *Schumann*. Oxford University Press, 2012.

The New Grove Composer Biography Series:

    Sadie, Stanley, ed. *Beethoven*. Norton, 1983.

    Sadie, Stanley, ed. *Haydn*. Norton, 1983.

    Sadie, Stanley, ed. *Mozart*. Norton, 1983.

    Sadie, Stanley, ed. *Schubert*. Norton, 1983.

    Sadie, Stanley, ed. *Early Romantic Masters*. Norton, 1985.

    Sadie, Stanley, ed. *Late Romantic Masters*. Norton, 1985.

Roseberry, Eric. *Shostakovich: His Life and Times*. Hippocrene Books, 1982.

Solomon, Maynard. *Beethoven*. Second Revised Edition. Schirmer, 1998.

Solomon, Maynard. *Mozart: A Life*. HarperCollins, 1995.

Swafford, Jan. *Johannes Brahms: A Biography*. Alfred A. Knopf, 1997.

Swafford, Jan. *Beethoven: Anguish and Triumph*. Houghton Mifflin Harcourt, 2014.

Todd, R. Larry. *Mendelssohn: A Life in Music*. Oxford University Press, 2003.

Historical and Cultural Background

THE NEW OXFORD HISTORY OF MUSIC SERIES:

Abraham, Gerald, ed. *The Age of Beethoven, 1790–1830*. Oxford University Press, 1988.

Abraham, Gerald, ed. *Romanticism, 1830–1890*. Oxford University Press, 1990.

Cooper, Martin, ed. *The Modern Age, 1890–1960*. Oxford University Press, 1974.

Wellesz, Egon, and Frederick Sternfeld, eds. *The Age of Enlightenment, 1745–1790*. Oxford University Press, 1973.

NORTON INTRODUCTION TO MUSIC HISTORY

Downs, Philip G. *Classical Music: The Era of Haydn, Mozart, and Beethoven*. 1992.

Morgan, Robert P. *Twentieth-Century Music: A History of Musical Style in Modern Europe and America*. 1991

Plantinga, Leon. *Romantic Music: A History of Musical Style in Nineteenth-Century Europe*. 1984.

PRENTICE-HALL SERIES:

Longyear, Rey M. *Nineteenth-Century Romanticism in Music.* Third Edition. 1988.

Pauly, Reinhard G. *Music in the Classic Period.* Fourth Edition. 1999.

Salzman, Eric. *Twentieth-Century Music: An Introduction.* Fourth Edition. 2001.

GENERAL BACKGROUND

Campbell, Margaret. *The Great Cellists.* Trafalgar Square Publishing, 1989.

Campbell, Margaret. *The Great Violinists.* Pavilion Books, 2004.

Magris, Claudio. *Danube.* Harvill Press, 1989.

Rosen, Charles. *The Classical Style: Haydn, Mozart, Beethoven.* Expanded Edition. Norton, 1997.

Rosen, Charles. *The Romantic Generation.* Harvard University Press, 1995.

Schneider, David. *Bartók, Hungary, and the Renewal of Tradition.* University of California Press, 2006.

Segel, Harold. *The Vienna Coffee House Wits.* Purdue, 1993.

As a footnote, I will state that it is impossible these days to ignore the Internet as a fact source. Its level of sophistication and accuracy of information is steadily improving.